The Province Beyond the River

"This city is a rebellious city, hurtful to kings and provinces, and that sedition was stirred up in it from of old. That was why this city was laid waste. We make known to the king that, if this city is rebuilt and its walls finished, you will then have no possession in the province Beyond the River."

Ezra 4:15–16

The Province Beyond the River

W. Paul Jones

The Upper Room
Nashville, Tennessee

The Province Beyond the River

Upper Room edition published in 1986.

Originally published by Paulist Press in 1981.

Cover Transparency: Frances Dorris
Cover Design: Roy Wallace
First Upper Room Printing: October, 1986 (5)
ISBN 0-8358-0546-8

Printed in the United States of America

TO KAUCHEMA COMMUNITY

Our impossible dream of liturgical
faithfulness in the midst of poverty ghetto

especially to
A/ C/ D/ E/ K/ P/ P/ R/ S/ S/ S/ W
and LBD

Preface

I was almost three months in a Trappist monastery before I realized how dangerous spirit life can be. And so it was a bit of a surprise when early one morning I wrote:

These monks in this place are subversives, not so much because of what they say or even think, but what they are.... In the midst of a culture of noise, these little white-robed men who like to play with bells choose silence; in a culture of work, they choose contemplation; in a culture of self-realization, they renounce the self; in a culture of achievement, they declare that the winner will be loser and only the loser winner; in a culture whose economy is utterly dependent on consumption, they insist on emptiness; in a culture structured by possession, they insist upon detachment; in a culture intoxicated by facts and education, they insist on ignorance as the basis of wisdom; in a culture of complexity they call us to the simplicity of willing one thing; in a culture intent on a high standard of living they insist on a high standard of life. Achievement versus grace; the exposure of the emptiness of fullness for the fullness of emptiness. The heart of this subversion is in planting within a person the appetite for silence. And once planted, once one tastes silence, and listening, and stopping, and being flooded by a Depth beyond all words, once one lets go so that one's hands are empty for the first time, once you do nothing, say nothing, think nothing, but just let yourself *be* in the midst of Capital Peak or a columbine field or Snowmass Creek or the mist of a morning valley—if you ever let it happen, it is all over for you. From then on, everything else seems insane.

Yet so many people today do seem to be searching for a life of prayer, or the "spiritual." And it is increasingly serious, for, recognized or not, it is reflecting a growing hunger for meaning in the midst of a modern life orphaned from mystery, ecstasy, depth, and interiority.

I am a Protestant theologian, training persons to be ministers. I have been schooled at the best universities, have taught at excellent posts, and have published in journals and books. Most of those who know me have been convinced that I know where I stand, theologically and otherwise, and my life style of identity with the inner city would seem to reflect significant "faithfulness."

Yet, despite all that, in a moment of rare self-clarity a year ago, I realized how much I am one of these searchers. My relation to God was inexcusably undeveloped, ill-practiced, ignorantly narrow, and laced with a strange and suspect resistance to "intimacy." If such characteristics described a marriage relationship, those involved would be on the borderline between being marriage counseling dropouts and candidates for divorce.

Since I have long been conditioned to "lead with my mind," my natural inclination to do a study of the "subject" of spirituality would simply permit me to escape my dilemma one more time. Consequently, in order to subvert my defenses and dilute my excuses, I took a sabbatical leave to transplant myself into a community whose entire reason for being is the very factor most derelict in my own life: prayer and the spiritual life. This would be no effort at escaping mental struggle or the intensity of my activist involvements; it would underlie these, in a pilgrimage for a grounding depth, for perhaps solace—in one word, integrity.

So this book emerges as the journal of my adventure—the

entry into a Trappist monastery high in the Rocky Mountains. It was written originally only for me, as the vehicle of my struggle, the struggle either into prayer for the first time, or at least into the primal honesty to get out and play my theological games no longer. What happened was of such a nature that I have been encouraged by others to share that pilgrimage.

It is for that reason that the journal is offered. It is simply the story of a wanderer. May others feel through my strange path the sharing of a soul-companion.

In the end, Dorothee Soelle put it well: "I am writing for my brothers and sisters in the hope of finding brothers and sisters. It is a part . . . of struggling with the dreadful experience that we are so few."

Since this book was never intended, it was necessary to negotiate the final form with the Abbot. It is understandable that misinterpretations, unduly negative connotations, and violations of privacy and confidences need to be eliminated. After all, the incredible beauty of the spirituality I have experienced is the openness to have me at the heart of their monastic *family* life, where love is not so much in spite of weakness but in the gift of courage to share it all, therein living the image of one who has already done so beyond anything that we can imagine. Whatever changes in the manuscript were negotiated, the honesty of the experience has been preserved, with a spirit of vulnerability that testifies eloquently to the very spirituality to which this book is addressed.

I wish to express my thanks to Diane Kenney with whom I sensed that Ché and Tanya, monasticism and art, liturgies and inner city rhythms, somehow belong together. To Patricia Gateley, whose rare feminist soul and artistic spirit are such that I trusted to her the manuscript to be critiqued and loved. To Caroline Whiting of Paulist Press whose editorial suggestions marked the sensitivity of a sister pilgrim.

To one (or more) gypsies of serendipity, who has (have) given absurd joy at the most unlikely junctures. To the monks of St. Benedict's, brothers indeed. To my friend Richard Shaull, one of the few theologians writing today worth being the recipient of my critical anger.

To Saint Paul School of Theology, a community of rare creativity, with whom I have known both crucifixions and resurrections, until it has become a near-home.

And finally to the secretarial pool of Saint Paul, who have typed for me far more than contract or energy allows—I think particularly of Jo Laffler, Betty Barton, Natalie Keirn, and Lydia Cantrill.

*The Province
Beyond
The River*

Wednesday, May 31

It is 5:30 P.M. I'm on my way west on a Trailways bus, out-running the rush-hour traffic gushing from Kansas City. All I have are two pregnant suitcases somewhere under me, and several aborted tomato sandwiches in a sack on my lap. Come as you are, I was told: the Trappist principle of simplicity means bringing enough worker shirts and blue jeans for ten days, plus one Bible, and a special shampoo, if you are fussy. That's about what I have, but I cheated. Twenty-one books hid among the socks. Surprisingly they turned out to be mostly poetry.

And so across the great plains we inch, stopping at least once at each crossroads town. But I need all the delay I can get, readying myself for the months ahead—having left everything, with countless goodbyes; I have twenty-four hours to purge a way of life. I am going to a Trappist monastery, high in the Rockies, to be a monk for three months. And what does it offer? I only dimly know, after having tried for months to explain my decision. Once I called it "testing the darkness." Some people walk into their strength; I learn best by walking into my weaknesses. I am a theologian—I spend my life reading, teaching, thinking, writing, about God. I am mind, and I am action, attempting some sort of faithful mix of the two. But I must be honest—*I have never experienced God*, not really. I am embarrassed by piety; I am ill at ease with those who thrive on God talk; I have no awareness of what one might mean by the "presence of God." What would one conclude about a person spending her whole life dissecting, analyzing, and advocating love, but who has never herself been in love? Yet of many of my colleagues as

3

with many of my students, I suspect what I suspect about myself—I am a professing Christian and a *functional atheist.*

Therefore, at this two-thirds mark in my life, I have decided to "test the darkness." Once and for all, will it be vacuous emptiness, or filling wholeness? I no longer trust myself, so I have chosen to go where I cannot manufacture excuses anymore—to those who profess, as their whole reason for being, the worship, meditation, and contemplation of God, without reserve. And if I find nothing? . . . I am prepared to risk it all.

One hour on the road—still holding on. Things forgotten. Oughts—dos—guilts—could haves, should haves, if only . . . It helped to offer candy to a little boy with a stuffed turtle. The turtle, evidently, ate it.

Storm clouds; time for a sweater. Rain, then hail around 10 P.M. So much is beginning to happen as I begin to "let go." Short night vigils in each small town as old men wait out the night at cafe counters, praying in their own worn way for morning's coming. I had not expected to find monks so soon.

Thursday, June 1

After the solace of the village night, we atoned with the rapids of the Denver freeway—fighting for time, space, status, once again, again, again . . . I am taken by the class difference between planes and buses: cocktail executives versus the brown-sack folk. Next to me an old woman was able to produce from a brown paper bag ingenuity capable of enduring any situation.

It's 11 A.M. now. The bus is climbing through the high mist, into the Rockies. Ragged, free, solitary bird, simple, raging white foam—spirit country. Temperatures dropping. Climbing. Popping ears. Still letting go, slowly. Higher still. Mountains covered with snow. As we reached the tunnel, it started to snow—a real blizzard.

The last miles down the western slope seemed endless. I was anxious now. Only a few of us were left on the bus. A last

4

farewell from the driver as I stood alone at a gas station that he thought was my stop. Nothing more. No monk, I was told, had been there that day. I was over an hour late. The station closed soon. Five unanswered calls to the monastery. No answer...

Then as the attendant locked the pumps for the night, my last dime conjured up a cheery voice with car promising to be there soon. But as I turned from the phone, there was a sun-worn face beside me, saying that he was going to the monastery too. Outside the closed gas station the face turned out to be an ex-priest, a self-professed exorcist into whom "the spirits he has deposed had returned to haunt." He (or they) spoke alternately of suicide and of being God Incarnate. Not soon enough Brother "A" arrived and embraced me warmly.

The three of us started the ascent, in a car created slightly later than the mountains. After at least an aeon we came out into the valley (3,800 acres, it turned out) rimmed with 13,000-foot mountains. There, in the center, embracing the earth as if in apology for being, was the monastery.

Suddenly I was unready. Chigger bites itching under one arm, the beginnings of a cold, an uneasy stomach, the exorcist bringing increasingly incoherent pontifications of doom from the back seat.

Too soon I found myself in a "trial" room in the infirmary, with an invitation to a Lebanese supper cooked by visiting missionaries, a lament that I had missed their unique Eastern-like liturgy, many warm embraces, a thoughtful glass of wine, and much conversation as a special way of observing this special occasion.

After doing dishes together, I returned to my room, surrounded by "the great silence." My preparation for sleep was made hard by dual news: the monks had just begun a new strict "natural approach" to their traditional vegetarian diet, filled with more "cons" than "pros"; and "so as to enjoy time for morning peace," they had made the new rising hour 2:45 A.M.!

I had imagined that this life would not be easy, but this is ridiculous.

5

Friday, June 2

2:45 A.M. is an unbelievably early hour to rise, even when one is irrationally eager. At 2:55 we began the "daily hours" with Vigils, the time of keeping watch in the darkness, as in Jesus' parable of the virgins and the lamps. We "awaited the kingdom," as all of creation is shadowed by the death of sleep. To be found faithful, white robed in the candled darkness. Chanting before the icons, two readings (one ancient, one modern), with meditative silence. Then the day's gospel, followed by prayer and a dismissal. It had sounded good when I read about it.

It truly was impressive; but I cheated. I went back to bed (they had encouraged me not to get up until Eucharist). Lauds (morning praise) was at 7:30 A.M. in the atrium to the chapel. This is one of the two central offices (along with Vespers); here time is sanctified by praising God's gift of one more dawn, symbol of Christ's victory over death. The primal chaos is overcome in light, as Lauds is followed in the chapel with the Eucharist— life as promised incarnate fullness.

Emotionally strange, intellectually understandable. But existentially, I couldn't find much for breakfast (each makes his own, whenever he chooses). So, hardly equipped, I was assigned to work with the novice, Brother "B". But before we had hardly begun, he went for a dentist appointment, leaving me feeling very alone in my first efforts at humility—disciplined scrubbing of disciplined rows of disciplined toilets.

Surprisingly, I finished early, and as a self-reward I became a child, poking around the basement with Christmas eve-like guilt. I discovered an excellent music room (piano, guitar, stereo, records), power tools, supplies, and endless storage rooms. In a way it was a basement of history—an undressed loom, half-made icons, once favorite books, once loved carving tools— memories, bits and pieces of monks who had come, and who had gone. Dusty remnants awaiting a new novice, a different time. Everything a person could imagine was there—someplace. At supper last night two monks were discussing what year this is.

One thought it was 1976, another 1978. But they soon conceded that it didn't matter much anyhow. I sensed my linear time beginning to curve on both ends.

This afternoon an unexpected liturgy began. I found myself emptying my pockets. It was a strange exercise in shedding the unnecessary. Into the bottom drawer went my precious appointment book (a bell will suffice here), my phone number book (talk is a low priority), then my keys (what is there to lock?), pen and pencil (memory is enough), my change (no need of money—I work here as I can, and use as I need), and finally my wallet (no need of identification to prove who you are). So equipped with a handkerchief and a new lightness, I went to lunch.

That was an experience too. The new diet is enough to keep one suspicious. The drink looked like French dressing, smelled like celery, and turned out to be carrot juice—"a must each day." And the totally vegetarian casserole, heated without cooking, well, that was a skirmish too. As I barely endured in silence, Br. "B" read from a history of the Cistercians.

I was given the afternoon off, just "to be." After the office of None (a 2 P.M. spiritual equivalent of a coffee break), I went for a two hour walk to "kill time," as I put it. I was unprepared. Through dandelioned meadows, over senile fences, up pastures which like green fingers probed into the aspened slopes. Then with a sudden fling three deer bounded across the path, up through the higher brush, until they paused, silhouetted on the ridge. Everything that ever was held its breath, and for a moment a veil was drawn.

It was an afternoon of sheer delight. I saw seventeen deer in all (I think some put in more than one appearance). But then it became "to much." Emerging from a thicket, I was face to face with a fawn. If the God I seek is the presence of mystery, I was on the threshold—eye to eye, deep to deep, a kind of ecstatic rightness—until courage wore thin. With a form that was sheer grace, she left.

It was late afternoon when I discovered the hermitage—an old log cabin with a red door. A bed, stove, lantern, chair. It seemed to symbolize an infinite regress. I retreated from my

7

world to be alone with nine others; and each of them retreats from his retreated world; and in the heart of the hermit there is the retreat from self, etc., etc. Intriguing.

Before supper Br. "C" thoughtfully (and apologetically) sought me in my cell, to explain how one prepared his own supper, especially in the light of the new diet. As it turned out, he was no convert to it. Above all his sadness was as cook—not being able to fry, bake, or season. "It is like being an aviator," he explained, "who can grease all the planes but not fly any of them." With obvious incredulity, he related the "miracle cures" and longevity made possible with the new approach; but his chuckled disbelief became apparent over bananas. They are the "miracle food." Last week the nine monks ate thirty-three pounds of bananas. "If that's what it takes," he confessed, "I'm not sure I want to live that long."

Left to myself and the huge kitchen, I floundered until the Abbot appeared. His wisdom may be the life-saving turning point in my stay—where they keep the eggs, and how to hard-boil one at this altitude. I knew then that in the months ahead my relation with eggs would become quite intimate.

Vespers at sunset: the offering up of our day to God. Thankful, tranquil, at peace ... until we chanted Psalm 137. Someone had gone through the Psalter and penciled out all of the "offensive" verses. In this case it was the human cry for violence. This "cleaning up" of reality offended me. But the final word came from an unexpected source. As we walked through the cloisters to our cells, the beloved, peace-loving cat gleefully trotted in front of us with a freshly killed ground squirrel. Evidently someone had neglected to censor his Psalter.

Saturday, June 3

I awoke at 2:45 A.M. for Vigils, surprised to find that I had been able to pray immediately before sleep and upon awaking. It was spontaneous, taking the form of simple conversation, the kind one might have with oneself, but it seemed different this time.

During the early hours I studied the history of monasticism, trying hard to distinguish anchorite and cenobite, and the uniquenesses of the various orders. It is incredible how much of this rich tradition has been lost to Protestants. I will have to work further on this, but at the moment (5:30 A.M.) staying awake is difficult enough. I will have to work out a better rhythm. Seemingly I need close to eight hours of sleep to be at my best, but I have been getting six.

Since Br. "D" (who is to supervise me) still has not returned to the monastery, Fr. "E" assigned me to "eliminate" six piles of dirt that had resulted from planting aspens in the yard. It was hard work, but it felt glorious to be out of doors. In fact I got a bit delirious—watched by snow capped mountains, and led by a wheelbarrow through millions of golden dandelions. It seemed strange that these flowers, the bane of suburbanites, should bring such joy to Trappists. Even Fr. "E", who had to make a quick trip to town for an allergy shot, was back in time to roam through the dandelions by twilight with the rest of us.

The monks are concerned about the annual summer "invasion" by tourists. The gatehouse (their gift shop one mile from the monastery) will not be reopened due to lack of personnel, but evidently that is not enough. Rumor has it that a gate will be built to keep all visitors away, except for daily Mass. The other tidbit is that on Tuesday an architect is coming to consider the possibility of a pond at the edge of the yard. I hope it will mirror the mountains.

Vespers closed with the Magnificat, in honor of Mary, who is particularly dear to Trappists. I was doing rather well (especially with the radical social change dimensions involved in the Magnificat), until I noticed that Mary in the lighted stained glass window before which we were standing, was perched on something very yellow. Although my mind kept saying that the artist probably was suggesting a quarter moon, my eyes could see nothing but Mary, astride a banana.

A hot shower for newly detected muscles gave opportunity to reflect on why I wanted so much to please the monks by hard work. Was I "earning" their graciousness towards me? Should it matter so much what others think of me? But it does. If only I could do well what I do, not needing to be appreciated—to give it as a gift.

At 6:30 P.M. we had song practice, preparing for what supposedly would be the well-attended Sunday Mass. I had fun singing and found it fascinating to observe, even here, how much competitive difference of opinion there was, even on such matters as tempo, rests, loudness, etc.

Sunday, June 4

2:45 A.M. was a *bit* easier today. Vigils were darkly warm, enfolding. A cup of coffee at 5 A.M. promises to be my salvation. I am finding it easier to pray if I regard it as talking to God as companion. But still I have to think about it—it is far from natural.

I am being drawn to Scripture for my reading—it is as though I have to come to terms with it if I am to be opened to such matters as contemplation. Leading, as I always have, with my mind, I located a book on Gospel parallels in the library. I began working through the basic differences between Mark, Matthew, and Luke. Is Jesus knowable within the differences, really? Also I decided to do regular readings in the various types of Scripture—Law (Deuteronomy), Prophets (Jeremiah), Gospels (Luke), Epistles (James). It was frightening to realize that I have never read the whole Bible, ever.

I was startled also when one of the secular readings during Vigils mentioned dreams as a major spiritual source. Yet I am rarely conscious of dreaming. Just that night, however, I became very aware of having had a dream, insignificant though it seemed.

By 4 A.M. the "cook" placed in the kitchen the newest diet

invention—seven uncooked grains with cut fruit, soaked overnight in juice. I will have to try it, sometime. I remain loyal to eggs for the time being. Lauds and Mass are later on Sundays— at 8:15 A.M. Not knowing what to do, I sat at the back. The chapel was full, with perhaps one hundred persons. Strangely my initial feeling was that my "home" had been invaded. This was followed by a new and unwanted feeling—that women don't belong here. Strange. I'll have to get in touch with that, since, ironically, I find the sexist language here needless and offensive. My hope is that I am beginning to sense a deep and rare sense of brotherhood, similar to the feminist discovering of sisterhood as a unique reality. Nice feeling!

The liturgy was pure, the music rich, and the Abbot gave the best homily that I was to hear that summer. He began, as I expected (and feared), with the issue of a personal virtuous life as the highest goal. Monastic homilies I had previously heard tend to move relentlessly into self-help suggestions and variations on the theme of obedience to law. So I was delighted when his thesis emerged as this: the greatest virtue is to know that one has none. Only when our hands are empty does God fill us. Although he did not use the term, it was a message of grace.

Sunday is the "sabbatical" day—being "without labor." But I was assigned eggery chores with Br. "A". (Chickens, it seems, are non-liturgical.) We gathered the contributions from five thousand chickens and placed them in a cooler. Actually the rhythmic repetition was fun; but I was haunted by the inhumanity (inchickenity?) of automated Auschwitz chickens, who only see natural light when they arrive, and then finally on their way to the Campbell Soup factory.

Lunch was a delight—uncontaminated food, good brothers, rain sweeping the roof, fog from the mountains fondly nuzzling the windows, and in the silence we listened to classical music. So fine.

The afternoon I spent reading the Bible. By evening I was developing negative feelings about Br. "D", who is to be my di-

11

rector. He has finally returned to the monastery, greeted me before Mass, but has said nothing more. A number of monks have given me "temporary" instruction on various things, indicating that when Br. "D" returns, he will fully instruct me. I am still uninstructed.

In my aloneness I am beginning to sense how each of us is a hermit, and it seems crucial to acknowledge this. Alone we are pulled into this world, alone we are pushed out of it. The feel of our inferiority, our finitude, is solitariness. Yet we deny this reality by living so much of our lives according to the expectations of others. It is urgent that I learn the responsibility of standing totally alone (before God?).

Vespers are early on Sunday, and then all of us go to the refectory together. The mood is quite different: informal, talkative, laughing, sharing. Evidently they used to have a special fellowship meal Sunday evening, but due to the new diet, each prepares his own. Consequently the fellowship now consists of the individual preparations together. Afterward some monks brought chairs into the kitchen, the Abbot brought us to order, and in a fun, relaxed way, we discussed the summer schedule for Sunday Mass. For the last several years the monks have discouraged tourists by moving Mass time earlier. After a new impasse, a compromise won: the Mass would be fifteen minutes earlier. What followed was a discussion of ingenious ways of discouraging worshipers from overstaying their tentative welcome. Decision making seemed to take forever, except on one issue: instant approval was awarded the Abbot for his idea of a cookout in the mountains next Sunday. How to do this with new dietary restrictions, however, turned the group to good natured despair when a roasted carrot on a stick evoked no excitement. We decided to fish this week; if they were biting, the menu was established. The mood would have been the envy of every fraternity. It was downright fun.

I noted that although decisions were jointly made, the Abbot's opinion was generally known before voting. I became aware of how young everyone was. The Abbot, in a loose blue sweater, resembled a gangly good-natured campus jock. I wonder how long it will be before the hard mountain life takes its toll?

At bedtime, a large fly was obviously breaking the rule of silence. But in this place, I found that I couldn't do what once I would have done with gusto—wop it! Ironically, by the time I gently caught him, took him down through the cloister, and set him free, he had dropped dead.

Monday, June 5

2:45 A.M. is still early. I now grudgingly believe it will remain so, by definition. The temperature dropped to freezing so that a little heat in the chapel was the motivation I needed. I find myself counting the days I have been here, wanting the time to go more slowly. I do not want to leave, or even think about leaving. I have hardly begun, whatever that means. We have been reading Morton Kelsey's *The Other Side of Silence* during Vigils. Several of the monks are uneasy about how critical he is of non-image prayer. This would especially undercut Eastern mysticism (such as Yoga and Zen) which some of the brothers here have found helpful. In fact, in response to my request of Fr. "E" for his favorite book on prayer, he recommended *Prayer* by Abhishikta nanda, a Benedictine who studied deeply Eastern understandings. I will read it, but will do so knowing that I must resist increasingly the temptation to read *about* prayer, rather than learn by plunging myself into it.

Today was egg day. On Mondays and Thursdays the monks go to the eggery, and with ingenious machinery the hens' whole vocation is processed into colored boxes recognizing "individual achievement." Appropriately I was placed at the end of the process, by the "merry-go-round," where the boxes come off the line, defying me as I scramble to catch them for packing in cartons. It was an unthinking task. Surprisingly, for that very reason, it was monastically delightful.

13

The monks were in good but different places, and when there was talking, it was a friendly joking. There was little instruction—I had to pick it up, and they trusted that I would. When the work was done, four of us sat, savoring the after-moments of a task well done, together. Fr. "E" took out a carefully hidden foil ball, and with the egg sanders as paddles, we played a game of hockey on the "merry-go-round." Halfway down the road home, it started to rain. We arrived at lunch, out of breath, covered with mud, but blessed with an abandonment usually reserved for children.

Br. "D" said that he still wouldn't have time to meet with me, until tomorrow—a bit disappointing, but that meant no work, and more time for reading. The only daily paper they receive for contact with the world is the *Wall Street Journal*. It is worse than I had imagined, without even major league ball scores as compensation.

With the discovery that the new diet discourages wine at meals, I am beginning to wonder if one can be too pure.

The schedule, as I have finally been able to memorize it, is this: 2:45—Rise; 2:55—Vigils; 7:30—Lauds and Eucharist; 9:15—Work; 12:30—Sext/Lunch/Dishes; 1:15—Siesta; 2:00—None; 2:30–4:30—Work; 7:00—Vespers; 8:00—The Great Silence.

I was pleased that at lunch a brother read an article from the *Christian Century* criticizing the Church of England and the Roman Catholic Church for their stands against women priests.

At None, I became aware that at worship I am still seated outside the circled chairs of the monks, where guests sit, and tonight at 6 there is a "community meeting" that doesn't include me. I am trying to think of something exciting to do while they meet without me, but my monastic imagination is rather primitive (I settled for a shower).

While preparing my supper, Br. "E" asked if he might speak to me. "I am pleased," he said, "that you seem to know how to use your time. Some people come here and within a day they are bored. Last month a monk came from another monastery and on Sunday afternoon he asked me what I was going to do. I said, 'Nothing, just go to my cell and be.' He could understand 'doing' but not 'being'—that is too bad." I told him I just hoped three months would be time enough. He winked. He understood. We were brothers.

The Vespers' closing psalm began: "Behold how good and pleasant it is when brothers dwell in unity."

Tuesday, June 6

The darkness was very cold again, but there was simple joy at 3:45 in sitting on a counter in the warm kitchen, reading Jeremiah, and holding a hot cup of coffee in both hands. At 4:55 from the library window I saw the first hint of dawn. Rather, I did not see it. The birds did, and I heard their seeing. Nothing loud or even sure. Just the hint of birds yawning, as they stirred to consider the day. In such a setting the poetry of Jeremiah became exciting. The lines stumbled over themselves with imagery—wandering, desert, mountain, lost sheep, wind, fire, terror, loneliness, abandonment, rest, remnant . . . And the faithful Jeremiah, called to prophesy against the very nation he loved, spat upon, imprisoned, abandoned in the mud of a deep cistern, threatened, beaten, captured—rejected as traitor—a hermit in the midst of many. As I finished the book, the birds were singing, insistently now, and light was touching at the tip of Mount Sopris. How can "sound" be so silent? Or silence speak so well? Jeremiah's integrity came at daybreak.

Increasingly the Eucharist is containing for me a strange joy. I seem to sense a presence in and through the breaking and sharing of bread. Fr. "E", in a brilliant red robe for the martyrs, embraced me movingly. We celebrate in the large chapel, standing around the table, serving one another.

My task this morning was to sweep and wet mop the cloisters (open hallways), novitiate (the room for training new monks, now used also as a chapter or community meeting room), the chapel, and the reading room. It had a comforting feel—home begins when one starts the unending and thankless task of keeping rooms clean. In the afternoon I began my apprenticeship to a vacuum cleaner.

This morning I received my first letter from home—with tears. I walked in the field. Br. "A" was watering aspen trees. He had dug them by hand, up on the mountains, evidently without encouragement from some brothers. He did this before they leafed, and though he daily watered them, he told me of two weeks of "agony" when he feared that his "friends" had died. He had volunteered to do something with the yard enclosed on three sides by the monastery. But he had been discouraged by disagreement among the monks. Evidently strong opinions ranged from seeded grass to letting the area be reclaimed by the sage brush. The fact that I had removed the piles of dirt and raked the rough spots seemed to make us brothers of the soil. As he watered and talked, the pronoun slowly became "we," he and I, and what we could do with this field in front of "home." I suggested that we fill in some bare spots by transplanting wild grass from the field that rumor prophesied might soon become a pond. He was excited. When I returned to the library I found two books—one on transplanting sod, the other on landscape gardening. I placed them in his mail box.

Just before supper, Br. "D" found me for our long delayed conversation. He was friendly, caring, direct, accommodating—but evidently overburdened with "too much." Among other things, I remember these in particular: after a week or so, if things go "right," I will be moved from the infirmary room into my own cell in the newly built monk's wing. Soon after that, when the community and I both feel right about it, a place will be set for me in choir for the offices. We walked through the monastery, getting a feel for its rhythm through its mechanics. I was assigned two hooks in the shower room for towels, a drawer for toilet articles, a box in the basement entry room as a locker for boots, hooks in the sub-cloister on which to hang my work clothes, a drawer for clean clothes, and an official mail box. There is a music room for monks only, which I will be permitted to use "carefully." "In enjoying what is available elsewhere, you may lose valuable time for that which this monastic community uniquely has to give." Makes sense. I was given access to supplies (toothpaste, stamps, etc.) as well as to any additional clothes that I might need. My gift was a list of rules, most of which I had come to know the hard way. They had to do with silence (listing nine areas where total silence is expected during the day, with total silence everywhere at night), entrances (not through the kitchen!), dish washing together after the noon meal, no snacks, ways to check out library books, when to eat breakfast, and singing in choir (quietly, please). The result of this orientation was a much better sense of belonging, especially to a "way of life."

As I prepared for bed, I looked out at the glistening mountain as the last rays of the sun teased the peak. Sopris. That was the name of a military man who was one of the first white men to enter these lands—and he dared to name it for himself. That mountain had a name before whites knew this continent existed—but I fear it may now be nameless. Somehow, either in reading or fantasy, I seem to remember the Indians using the word silver in regard to her. And so it will be—Silver Mountain. What strength—she will be there, whether I sleep or whether I awake. "When I look to the mountains . . ."

Wednesday, June 7

Morning risings are becoming easier (not easy). It is still the Eucharist that is particularly feeding. During prayers there were intercessions for wisdom, patience, justice, and lack of prejudice in the issue of "women priests." Also for fairness in deliberations with the I.R.S. (I learned later that monasteries do not now pay taxes on religiously used property and do not pay salaries. There is to be a meeting of monasteries later this summer, as the latest rulings seem to be going against them.) The Eucharist seems to be something of a repetition of the Incarnation. We are incorporating "very God" into "very self." The words of the Magnificat are appropriate: "He has regarded my low estate . . . He who is mighty has done great things for me." This echoes the words presently used: "O Lord, I am not worthy to receive you, but only say the word and I shall be healed."

During the early hours I found myself doing something strange. As I sat in the library, staring off into space, I heard the door knob turn. Instantly I grabbed a book, pretending to be reading. How ingrained it must be in me that to be "caught" doing "nothing" is a weakness, bordering on sin. Life is doing, or resting from much doing for the sake of even more doing. But here it is different. In doing "nothing," what I am doing is "being." It is enough, if only I can remember!

My joy for the day was in being assigned gardener. A beautiful blue sky day. Mountains. Morning sun. I watered trees, gathered stones from the garth (I was told that this was the official name for our dandelion patch), repaired hoses, trimmed the edge of the cliff, picked up dead branches. In the afternoon I loaded the "junk" into the pickup and took it to the dump. What is it about driving a pickup on a rare day on a back country road all by yourself? Well, that's what I felt, even in being gloriously caught in a mountain shower as I unloaded.

There is a young woman making a retreat at the guest house; she comes for morning prayers, Eucharist, and Vespers. I have to admit, she makes prayer difficult.

Had another short talk with Br. "A", in which he told me of his favorite walks. Evidently there are two more hermitages. One is on a high mesa miles away. The other is an old trailer, high on the hillside overlooking Monastery Valley. Fr. "E" pulled it up there with the caterpillar. Br. "D" said of it, "If you ever go up there, you will never want to come back."

We all had supper together, with three tables pulled together in family style. I was told by Br. "D" to watch my watch, and at 6 to "get lost." They are going to have a meeting of some sort. I did my laundry. They were a half hour late for Vespers. I found that I had resentment, even though with my mind I understood. I needed sleep in order for the feeling of rejection to go away.

Thursday, June 8

I got up in the middle of the night with a severe headache—it made me aware of how many I have been having lately.

I find myself praying spontaneously when I awaken, using "rich" language that I had never been comfortable using before. I don't know where that's coming from, or what it means. These were the best Vigils for me thus far. Despite the terrible hour, I was alert, internally warm, caring. I experienced a gentle imagination, flowing with the psalms or readings, doing my thing when I felt inclined. It all fit together with a happy rightness. But immediately afterward I found myself concerned about my life in the city—but that must wait. It is far too soon.

I admit a mischievous delight over the fact that the Abbot was late for Vigils.

This was egg day. Previously I had seemed to be doing work with others in mind, probably for approval. Today I seemed to be doing it because it was to be done. In the afternoon, working on the garth, I found I was doing it simply to beautify the place—for its own sake. I hope this shift can continue.

During the siesta my walk provided a chance discovery of the cemetery, with two graves of monks I had known—one very twisted in body, the other a vibrant black monk, who soon after being ordained drove a jeep by accident off a mountain cliff. Here were the remains, hidden among the sagebrush, and two simple crosses with names, serving both as a reminder and as a perch for miscellaneous birds. Fifty feet away, strangely, I found a third grave, of a woman. Later it was identified as that of a gracious friend of the monastery, who on her deathbed prevailed upon the Abbot for monastic space. She told others he had said yes. He hadn't. She died. He graciously obliged. Beautiful.

It seemed time for me to do something more disciplined about that for which I came. In the late afternoon I took my reading seriously and chose a mantra. This is a word or phrase (it need not have meaning but should) that is repeated over and over. Supposedly two things can happen: 1. A centering of the mind to a fine focus, until everything of distraction is dismissed. The centered mind slows its pace until it becomes "turned off." This is pure emptiness, pure being, at peace and unity. The mantra, evidently, strengthens the will so that one can do it by choice. 2. "Praying without ceasing"—the mind can continue this repetition "automatically." I suppose this is similar to secular life in which a popular song can haunt one. This establishes a *habitus* ("habit"), a disposition toward Presence. This method may be very useful, for I am discovering that the primary enemy of prayer is forgetfulness.

Mass on Thursday is at 6:30 P.M. in remembrance of the Last Supper. It is simple, a family style event in the atrium, with everyone sitting on chairs about the common table.

Friday, June 9

I awoke very tired and very stiff from digging yesterday, so I was pleased with my capacity to will two things: (1) to will awakeness and alertness at Vigils; (2) to will to go back to bed when they were over. Instead of feeling guilt, I felt wisdom. At 6:30 A.M., while preparing breakfast, two young people, evidently on retreat, came to the kitchen, found some corn flakes somewhere, and ate. Self-righteously I watched them eating such an "unclean" thing—toasted cardboard. Evidently this diet thing is making more of an impact on me than I had hoped.

A book on the canonical hours helped me empathize more with the monastic sacralizing of time. The day is divided into eight blocks of three hours each, with an office (service) to define each with Christian meaning. These form the anatomy, together with the church year, of the monk's life. Space, on the other hand, is sacralized by sacramentals, objects of taste, sound, sight, touch, and smell that particularly evoke awareness of the Gospel rhythms. This reading enfleshed intellectually what I have been experiencing emotionally.

Matins and Vespers begin and close the day, while Vigils mark the alone waitfulness of the night under promise. The "little hours" are numbered from the moment of the daily "resurrection." Prime (1st hour) is the time of joint planning of the day's labor in remembrance of the saints whose day will mark as models our own; Terce (3rd hour) is the mid-morning "spirit-break," in which the descent of the Spirit at Pentecost is in polarity with the time of cross building; Sext (6th hour) is the pause at noon's heat, when the remembrance of the crucifixion hours parallels the fatiguing dominance of the purely physical; None (9th hour) images the convergence of Christ's death and our own call to endurance within the declining day—"S/he that shall endure to the end . . ." And then Vespers ("evening"), happening at the appearance of the evening star, the offering up "eucharistically" of the works of our hands as did Jesus at the hour of the last supper, in foretaste of our final banquet home together at last. It is the "feel" of "turning into the driveway," of laborers home from the harvest, of a glass of wine together at fireside. And finally Compline ("complete"), the Gethsemane hour before sleep, making one's peace with one's brothers, relinquishing one's hold on life in dying unto the Lord—"Into your hands we commend our spirit . . . May the Almighty Lord grant us a peaceful night and a perfect end." The Great Silence begins enwrapped in the everlasting arms, unless with the coming of Lauds God might see fit to grant us the glorious gift of one more day of life.

I have picked up tidbits of vital information as I worked. For example, one asks permission always, and of the right person. There is a certain possessiveness of task, so that one does not return to the paint room paint cans that have been sitting for six months on the floor of the boot room (even though one is told to clean the boot room) without checking with the brother in charge of the paint as well as the "boot room" monk. Likewise, one may give opinions, but you still do precisely as you are told. The novice underscored such "wisdom"— in his one and a half years here one of the hardest but most necessary lessons was obedience. "I have a strong ego, and I know good ways of

21

doing things; but I must do them a certain way because it is what the Abbot wants done."

I discovered that there is a name for each room, some official, some informal. Today was like a game, discovering rooms where I couldn't imagine them existing—rooms through rooms into rooms: icon making room, loom room, swill room, treasury room, carpentry room, packing room, etc., etc.

At lunch we heard two articles from *America,* a Jesuit publication. They were disturbingly "right-wing." One concerned the "bloodiness" of Cuba's unwarranted aggression in Africa. The other claimed that preferential treatment of previously discriminated minorities is wrong unless the majority of whites vote willingly to be themselves discriminated against. I had to go for a long walk to get this out of my system. I had not expected such "patriotism" among those whose commitment I had thought would be so uncompromisingly monotheistic—whence forth then cometh idols? In a conversation later with the monk who chose and read it, the good-natured response was that he wanted some exposure to such issues. Another monk confessed that he just smiled at such a position and didn't think anymore about it.

During the afternoon three signs were hung on the newly constructed archway at the Gatehouse. The first says, "Stop Ahead." The next, "Do not go beyond this point." The third indicates a telephone that can be used for emergency, the founding date and purpose of the monastery, and the time of daily Eucharist. Their posting created noticeable happiness with the monks: while remaining open in policy, they are pulling back in privacy, resisting the inroads on the solitude and silence which is their raison d'être. I understand, agree, and yet believe that they have a mission. Their mission is to be, yet their being must be known as possibility for those of us deprived (at least through ignorance) of this essential dimension.

For the first time I heard music from the music room. The record selection turned out to be a Strauss waltz, "It's a Long Way to Tipperary," "Over There," and "Ave Maria." Atonement was forthcoming, however, when, as I watered trees at sunset, I heard Br. "A's" "orchestra" in the guest chapel. Somehow he had collected an organist, a guitarist, and several violinists from the monastery and nearby neighbors. When they left, I quietly played the piano.

There was another closed community meeting, but at Vespers Br. "J" was finally remembered. As I prepared for bed I realized that here, as everywhere, we are dealing with human idiosyncrasies; but as far as I can tell, there are no locks needed, everything is held in common and equally available for us, and there seem to be no significant problems. Economic sharing, in some contexts, seems to be both real and desirable.

My closing thoughts for the evening were serious ones. I have been here over a week. I am still happy and excited. But it is precisely this sense of community and the meaningfulness of the liturgy that may be keeping me from the darkness. It is a total environment, a forming context. Thus "God exists" because to be in this community is to be shaped inevitably by that informing assumption. Here it *is* so, and to be here is to taste what it would be like to be so. But the facts of the matter are that in my non-work time I am involved in *reading*, not praying. And quite honestly, the precise differences between prayer, meditation and contemplation are all blurred to me. My latest reading is the favorite suggested by Fr. "E" (Nanda). It is delightful—clear, precise, personal, practical. I'm beginning to understand it, but *I am not doing it*—I am attending liturgies where it is being done. I went to bed discouraged.

Saturday, June 10

The morning began even worse. Right after Vigils I found a number of letters in my box. They were welcomed. It was good hearing from friends that I am cared for—so much so, in fact, that I began writing letters. Before I was done I had writ-

23

ten nine. The last letter I opened was from a friend whom I have known and worked with for years. While in the monastery, I agreed to keep in touch, as she was working on spiritual life and wanted to share her progress. She wrote five pages, sketching graphically her spiritual experiences from childhood to the present. She has had numerous experiences of the sensed "Presence of God," the comforting "nearness," the immovable "ground" when things went wrong. While she is dissatisfied, at least she has something with which to begin. But by contrast, *I have never even experienced God.* I can talk about all kinds of doctrines, but at rock bottom, in the sense in which she speaks— NO! I walk alone. The closest to it is the silence I experience here, the booming silence flooding my aloneness so that it is not lonely. What am I doing here? I haven't even tried—it is as if there are scars against doing it. Resistance coupled with not knowing how or even what. The more of her letter I read, the more angry I became. The professional thinkers have made it all so complex, learned, varied, pluralistic, hierarchical. Consequently one is afraid even to try. One needs a three-year course and a lifetime of total commitment to the task. I felt angrier. Without knowing it, my mind was now a thousand miles away, in the city. It was as though through these letters I had squandered what I thought I was beginning to have.

At lunch there was played a tape lecture by a nun, explaining to her sisters what it had meant to take a six-month sabbatical in the ranch house here at the monastery. Two things struck me—one was her agony of soul in returning to the noise and pace of the city, struggling with relating "wilderness and metropolis." But second, she spoke of her conversations with Protestants on this subject. Protestants, she concluded, were outstanding in activism, but without any tradition for solitude and aloneness. Her key discovery was that spirit life is born of silence, and that without the monastic model this dimensional fact of all of life is squandered; indeed, the loss is not even known, and the vehicle for its recovery is labeled as weakness. Perhaps I was not escaping the darkness after all.

Sunday, June 11

During Vigils I came to realize what I *have* really experienced. As far back as I can remember I have had a metaphysical longing, a craving so deep that it *cannot* be filled, or at least not with anything more than temporary slaking. Yes, I know not the presence, but I do know, oh do I know, *the impossible absurdity of the absence.* Perhaps this is the pure emptiness which is all we can bring before the God implied by the haunting vacuum. Our greatest perfection, said Soelle, is our deepest lack: the need for God. This is what Chesterton meant by feeling homesick at home.

For the next three hours I read Scripture—it was as though I couldn't read it quickly enough. I read from Genesis, Jeremiah, Hosea, Mark, Romans, Corinthians, and James. I was fed, filled—and I paused, and spoke, as if in conversation with God, the biblical phrases flowing in richness. "I take delight in your word."

I did my chores but that did not seem to matter. I became so excited that I began to write—and the ideas flowed. They have yet to be worked out, systematized, but at this point one beginning insight was that there is a very real difference between Eastern and Western approaches to the life of prayer and the spirit. Presently the tradition of the Christian West is so flooded by Eastern thought that there is confusion. But only as a Protestant am I robbed of tradition; within the Roman Catholic tradition it is almost pick and choose, so much being up for grabs.

Yet rather than being brought to despair, I was elated. I wrote, did research, trying from the experience of craving to simplify the Christian spiritual options. By the time Sunday liturgy came I was without breakfast and a bit indignant over the interruption. But it was all right—for I knew again why I was here. And I knew that the next step was to clarify options, so that the life of spirit could be a practicing of that which brings to living focus the theology that is me. I could now dismiss the tendency to be inhibited by what I didn't know about the varying spiritual exercises developed by others out of their own pilgrimages. The Eucharistic liturgy spoke of "the only Son of God." This suddenly made strange contact with me, an only child. It was from such loneliness/aloneness that Jesus entered the life of prayer. Things are beginning.

The homily today was repetitive, unsure, and without clear focus. In most Protestantism, to have inept or even mediocre preaching would be to perpetrate genuine spiritual violence on a congregation. But today the Eucharist that followed redeemed the sermon. One truly has to work hard to ruin the liturgy. And with imagination . . .

My Sunday chores were to help in the kitchen, preparing lunch and the cookout. Since yesterday afternoon one could feel the eagerness—monks looking at the sky, uneasy about a heavy wind that developed in the late afternoon, checking the barometer periodically, looking for dew on the grass—but despite all ill omens, by Mass time the weather was clear. The afternoon would be beautiful, and everything was "go" for the fish fry.

Our lunch, eaten quickly to the music of Tchaikovsky's Sixth Symphony (the "Pathetique" hardly matched our mood), was typical of Trappist fare at its best—steamed broccoli and carrots, home-made bread, orange juice, lettuce salad, milk, and fresh pineapple. By 2:00 we were packed in the jeep and pickup, and with excited shouts headed for "the high country." We traveled for one hour, but at 3-5 miles an hour we really didn't go far. I "sat" in the back of the pickup with the Prior; he told me about each neighbor and each mountain, both equally his friends.

We arrived at the top of the world, 160 acres and a summer home owned by a banking family from New York, now partly relocated in Aspen—used only occasionally, but available to the monks. Over a stream, around the home, and there—a panorama of Capital Peak and Mount Daly together—grandeur, rugged stone face, snow draped. For the first time I experienced the rare genius of a Trappist picnic—no small talk, no frisbees, just a time decided upon for regathering (5:30) and then each of us

26

went his way, "to that spot which is particularly yours, in which to be." Most of us took a book, several took folding chairs, one took a nap. I followed the stream, up through the towering white stemmed aspens. It was a cathedral, with sun piercing the green leafed arches. Forty-five minutes later, up a final rugged path, and I broke out onto a beaver pond, patiently being filled by a waterfall. To the left, 14,000 feet high, were the peaks—spirit companions. I had brought a book on contemplation. It remained unopened, under a tree where I sat—just sat.

Somehow the beauty of this place—it can only be enjoyed. And can it be that through us, God enjoys? It is as if through such joy that creation comes to know itself, and in so knowing knows God. The joy of being utterly alone and not lonely. All I could do, my sacramental act, was to take an orange from my pocket, peel it gently, and eat it, slowly, piece by piece. During the walk back every sense was engaged—sound (water, wind, birds), smell (evergreen, grass, wildflowers), touch (wind, rock dirt, bark), sight (indescribable), taste (wild grape ends). Then together we charcoaled fresh trout, adding potato salad, lettuce, beer and wine. It was genuine fun—laughter, appreciation, sharing. (Somehow in the face of such mountains I privately felt totally unclean to recognize this as private property.)

Thirty trout later, with the sun down, the wind up, and the cold setting in, we took to the trucks. I was surprised when we went only halfway home. Instead we stopped at the summer house of a restaurant chain owner from Denver. There we had a birthday party for Fr. "E," complete with candled cake, home-made ice cream, and home-made liqueur. A mellow, laughing time—I would call it the fellowship of fond remembering. "Remember when . . .?" After the dishes, we started home, the night wind freezing us in the back of the pickup. When the few remains that remained were back in the monastery kitchen, the Abbot announced that because it was so late, we would sleep in tomorrow. Never did I think that I'd ever regard "sleeping in" as being 5:30 A.M.—but just then I did. Shivering to get warm in bed, I remembered what Fr. "F" (a visiting monk from another monastery) said at the party—this monastery is unique in its informality and family-like style, everyone on a first-name basis. At his monastery, everything is formal: the Abbot is always "Reverend Father." This place is unique.

Monday, June 12

The experience of beauty yesterday drove me to seek in art and creativity models for understanding life in the spirit. I spent several hours looking at paintings. I was taken by the loneliness of the great artists—e.g. Rembrandt, Michelangelo. But above all I perceived art as providing various graspings of reality which could serve as visual models for those experiences which compositely we call Spirit. The logos, ontic structure of a Cézanne, the passionate driving spirit of a Van Gogh—these both are spirit life, mysteriously crying out for each other. Exciting— so much so that it seems as if more than one lifetime is needed to experience all that I want, and at least as many more lifetimes to write.

I find that I look forward to egg day, primarily because of the one-half mile walk to the eggery. I would wish for all persons, once before they die, a walk on such a mountain road at sunrise. I feel as if I'm in a parade, as ground squirrels on either side pop their heads from the holes and squeak (a Te Deum?).

The brother in charge of the eggery had a few harsh words to say when I was trying to be helpful. Perhaps it is because I have not felt any harsh words here that I found the hurt to last, even into the next day.

This afternoon was "graduation day"—I made it. I was invited to move my few possessions into the monks' wing and was given my own "cell." The price, of course, was the "privilege" of vacuuming the floors of all the cells. Then I spent several hours letting my room speak. There were two pieces of furniture to place—a bed and a desk. I finally settled for making one side of the small room clear, as a vista to the sliding glass door to the outside, with the desk facing those doors, looking out on the garth and the 10,000 dandelions. I fell in love with the room—it is home. The delicious joy of little things.

Tuesday, June 13

There was a beautiful darkness in my room after Vigils. I became aware how important is the basic informing image through which one "perceives" God. For most of us these images are unconscious, unrecognized, pluralistic. But their informing power in our perception and action is far deeper than we realize. I meditated on this, trying hard to detect how I operated. My image of God at this moment seems evoked by the motion of "gathering unto him/herself enriched." The words conjured up are "enfolding," "including," "embracing." These are the motions of eternity. The resulting image I have for the self is that of standing strong on the ground, toes wrapped in the dust, breathing fully the strength of the earth. Each person seems to crave this embracing oneness, but it is rare that one breaks through. The craving is blocked, the yearning overloaded, even to the point of short-circuiting. I find this dramatically focusing for me in the Eucharistic image—offering up and receiving back enriched, reconstituted, refined, again and again in cosmic rhythm.

Applying this image to other recent thoughts, I perceived the craving deep within me as being for *creativity*—and its meaning is known only through the act. So perhaps it is with God—not as an engineer builds rationally, intellectually planning a world, but God as artist, dreaming reality into being, fondling it into a life of its own. From this image prayer becomes discernment: waiting in the presence of being, sensing in silence the yearnings of creation together, as sister, related in the birth pangs of commingling agony. One does not know such things. It is a matter of being called—to a promise, by dream, by vision—lived, shoved, haunted, lured—a person possessed, a woman pregnant—the tortured ones. And so the life of almost every

29

great artist—possessed by a demon who is the Spirit, driving us to hope as the coming Kingdom thrown against the Nothingness surrounding and creeping at everything that is.

Perhaps there are two kinds of "possessed" ones—those seized by and for the earth—the artists, as it were. And those possessed by the self for the within—the mystics. I am the former, I would suppose. Yet I prayed for "infused contemplation"—if only ... to be embraced with the earth in God. The difference may be in the tense—is it so, or is it to be so?

In repairing fences with the novice, I shared my tendency at times to be mischievous here (e.g. to send a purple plastic egg through the machinery), or to see the absurd moments with a chuckle. He couldn't identify with it at all. He could only think that it meant telling jokes or playing games, and he saw no place for these. "Perhaps," he said, "being new at this I am super serious." With the older cook, however, I sense a spontaneous, fun-loving good-naturedness—he understands what seriousness requires.

I learned that the way one joins the monastery is through several visitations as an "observer," usually for several days, maybe a week. There is such a person here now for two weeks, his sixth visit. Today he requested entrance, beginning in the fall. The Abbot, and perhaps others, pushed him hard—why he thinks he is called, what he expects from it, etc. If all seems satisfactory, and the community votes yes, he is sent to a psychiatrist for a thorough examination. As it was explained to me, this strenuous life of the spirit is only for the strong, and it is better at the beginning that one understand this, and enter not as an escape or a compensation, but as a call. They are clear that the original desert fathers and mothers went to the wilderness not to escape, but to do battle—the desert is the citadel of the demons. It makes one wonder if to be a secular monk in the city would not today be the best equivalent of St. Anthony of the desert.

I was to meet in the library after Mass and then at None with the guest master for my daily work schedule. For the last several days, however, my contact has been through the novice who has received notes from him. Strange.

At noon the Abbot left for a week-long meeting in San Francisco. In saying farewells, he indicated that he wanted to get together with me when he returns. I was surprised when, asked how I was doing, I replied immediately: "Really, really well." And I felt tears in my eyes, sufficient to turn quickly to my afternoon work of repairing range fences.

I was pleased to find a letter from *The Christian Century* indicating that they would publish my correspondence regarding the Marxist-Christian Conference in Philadelphia. I tried hard to relate that part of my life to what I was presently about. There was tension—yet both are full and genuine parts of me and, I believe, the Gospel. Merton's last speech before his death suggested that it was in the monastery that Marx's communal vision is possible. I remembered also that Braaten once said that Christianity without apocalypticism and Marxism without transcendence are two heresies needlessly fighting each other. I am beginning to sense this.

Wednesday, June 14

In the early hours I worked on something that I have wanted to do for some time: to develop some short basic offices of the day—ones that others might use. I developed a working draft of Vigils, Lauds, Vespers, and Compline. I'm basically pleased, and am using them personally.

More and more I am being saturated by Scripture, and have vowed to finish reading the entire Scripture this summer. Already I have read nineteen books. There is something positive about reclaiming my Protestant heritage. In reading Exodus, I recalled Daily Vacation Bible School, as a boy, in which we made an actual model of the desert tabernacle. I got excited, checked out the size of a cubit (from elbow to finger tip—about one and a half feet) and discovered that the tabernacle was about as long as a football field is wide. I was tempted to pace it off outside, putting in stakes to indicate the holy of holies. Thus far I have settled for drawing a picture. I am impressed with the sacrificial center of the Old Testament and the new possibilities this provides for depth understanding of the New Testament Eucharist. This Scripture saturation is making prayer richer, for in speaking to God the language now flows—I pray in and with tradition, as if I were praying for and with the church, and the church prays through me.

But there is also a negative side. After reading especially Exodus, Leviticus, Numbers, and Deuteronomy, it is hard to keep liking God and Israel. While supposedly we are to identify with God in "his" struggle with Israel's unfaithfulness, I am stunned by God's sexism and his bloodthirstiness. The two seem related, and they are staggering. To please God Jael drives a tent peg through the head of King Sisera. In obedience to God, leaders lie and break promises in order to win. God commands: "Kill every male among the little ones, and kill every woman who has known man by lying with him. But all the young girls who have not known man by lying with him, keep alive for yourself." Not just once or twice—the books are filled with it. On the pages of the Book of Numbers in my Bible, for sanity's sake, I had to write: "This is mass murder." I cannot like Moses or his God! At times, God is like a little kid; the people do not do what he wants, so he zaps them—fire, plague, bees, famine. And above all he holds the supreme threat that they will never get to see the promised land. Threat after threat, despite his covenant. And his laws—I am overwhelmed by how many of them have, as penalty, being stoned. Killing as the religious way of life.

I went to bed overwhelmed by all of this. My quasi-conclusion was that religion is the last threshold against madness in the face of an absurd world and its "god." Insane with and insane without—one chooses one's insanity.

Br. "A" sang with guitar for Lauds, and we had Tchaikovsky's Violin Concerto "for lunch." This inspired me to speak to Br. "A" and we will get together, probably today, to write some music. Related, I am finding myself relinquishing my "oughts" and being led by what "feels" fitting to do. One pays a price for this, I guess, not the least of which was at Eucharist, when during the Lord's Prayer I observed my obliviousness: I had on a red shirt, orange socks, and yellow tennis shoes. I trust that God chuckled with me.

My face is browning like the earth. That feels right.

During Vespers we began reading an article on celibacy by Henri Nouwen. Celibacy is a witness, in the midst of an age craving relationships and totally open intimacy, of a holy and inviolable space in each of us. It cannot be filled by others, and we should not try. I believe as we read more he will say calmly what I feel intensely—this is the center from which flows that craving which cannot be filled by other than God. Each attempt to fill it otherwise becomes not only idolatry; it become frustration unto violence.

I "borrowed" a small clipping from a brother's plant and am trying to root life in my cell. Last night I picked up a twisted root shape—they, together with a red apple, are on the desk with me.

Thursday, June 15

A day of reflection. This is the end of my second week here. The stay has been creating a base. But I am restless to test the real darkness, as it were. I have largely been involved in reading, liturgy, work, and community. Prayer itself is hardly beginning, and I detect in myself yet a deeper resistance than I once thought.

My task was to clean the new cell wing. I am finding, to my delight, that I am almost able to work for its own sake and for my satisfaction, irrespective of the approval of others.

Friday, June 16

At Vespers last night there was a phrase from Psalm 87 that became important to me during meditation at Vigils: "Friend and neighbor you have taken away; my one companion is darkness" (v. 19). What is emerging is the idea of "companion prayer." It begins in solitariness as pure silence, which one may come to experience as pure potential for God (not of God), tasted as craving. The answer is not unity, or absorption, or self-loss. These ultimately would be a negation of me, a declaration that the craving is illusory, illicit, or unfounded. If the craving is substantial, it is the validation of me *in my emptiness*.

Thus what issues from the Christian faith is the revelation of Emmanuel, "God-with-us," God's assumption of humanness for God's self, and thus its thoroughgoing affirmation. This constitution of relationship as foundational (God *and* me) points toward the fundamental difference between East and West. Prayer, not mysticism, is central; and the nature of prayer is companionship. I read Br. Lawrence in this connection. His daily prayer was: "I beg thee to grant me the grace to remain with thee and to keep thee company; but that it may be the better done, my Lord, work with me, receive my labors and possess all my affections." Two things emerge: the image of "keeping company" with God, and, second, the centrality of that form of prayer which in so much writing is made elementary, as only a first step—"diffused prayer." This is prayer intermingled with other activities and therefore not regarded as "pure" (i.e. formal). But companion prayer is Emmanuel relationship in the *midst* of daily existence. It is the reverse of much tradition—it is not going apart in order to be with God where he is in purity, but our being discovered by God where God has chosen to be with us in *our* time space. This may be why Barth abandoned the idea of eternity, insisting instead on our time and God's time, interpenetrating.

Helpful is Bonhoeffer's idea that the Christian no longer sees anything nakedly, but now literally with Christ as mediator. That is, one no longer sees just Jack or Sally, but literally

34

perceives each as the "one for whom Christ died." So the mountains and the land. This is a matter of actually "beholding" through new eyes. Conversion is seeing all things in the resurrection of "the first time." Thus the *life* of prayer is its development as *habitus*, of so practicing that it is rendered a disposition, one's second nature—actually, a new nature. The pianist practices daily to make playing second nature, until one *is* Bach and Bach invades her; so with Christian existence. This is what the practice of prayer is all about—rehearsal so as to be able to see everywhere. Thus "pure" prayer is more rehearsal than "performance," rather than the other way around. Perhaps this is what Ignatius meant in contrasting "apostolic" with "monastic" spirituality. "Monastic" centers in the alone silence of enfoldment in God—peace, reunion, restoration, the inward journey into God. "Apostolic" centers in the providential God who intersects each moment of time with possibility and calling, the honing of the spirit within to discern more faithfully the presence and the luring of the Spirit without, the outward journey with God moving toward the outer edge. Both, it would seem, form a necessary whole.

The process begins when the darkness becomes Companion. Normally, to think is to dialogue with self (I–me) in a stream of consciousness of self to self. But in the transforming process of conversion, consciousness becomes no longer self to self, but self to alter-self, i.e., Emmanuel. In Lawrence's sense, prayer must have at its heart "familiarity"—the companion closer to me than breath itself, than I to myself. This is the very transformation of consciousness, for which the name is "prayer without ceasing." Such "conversation with," as a new mode of consciousness, gives rise to a new sense of providence: as Ram Dass said, "Once you know that God knows everything (about you), you are free." What more does the Incarnation declare than God's promise that "we are in it together"?

Br. Lawrence again: "Throw ourselves recklessly into the arms of infinite mercy." "The greatest glory one can give to God is to mistrust his own strength entirely and to confide himself completely to his protection." It is a "filial confidence in his providence, a total and universal abandonment of oneself into his hands, without worrying what would become of one after death . . ." Life as the cosmic mutuality of companionship. But it is not only for its own sake but for all. "God with" gives the basis for "perceiving in," for discernment, for detecting as midwife what is yearning to be realized everywhere. To see with God is to behold all through the very eyes of promise, and thus as a call to concrete co-creativity. "Action with" because of "consciousness with."

Put another way, one is drawn from past and future to the here and now, the present of the Presence, and it is here that life as prayer has its excitement—to live on the yearning edge of immediacy.

Enough for now. It is painful, however, to realize that while I may be coming to "know" all this, I am not really doing any of it.

In my Scripture reading, God is still "at it." In First Samuel, he has just removed his blessing and presence from Saul so that he will fall as king. Why? Because in a bloody battle, Saul saved the rival king and some of the better flocks from destruction. And in prophesying against Saul, what did Samuel, the great prophet of the Lord, do, because God commanded it? After "Agag came to him cheerfully, Samuel hewed Agag in pieces before the Lord in Gilgad" (15:32-33).

Because the office of None had become a perfunctory thing done dutifully only by two or three monks, we tried today the office as a one-half hour period together in which we centered in on silent meditation. Almost everyone was there—it is an interesting alternative to the secular coffee break.

Saturday, June 17

Outwardly, this was a day of work: building fences on the range. But internally, it was a day of excitement regarding prayer. I tried to put "companion prayer" into practice. It will be incredibly hard, since I am attempting to undo forty-eight years of "practice" in I–me consciousness. For a strongly self-directed person like me, this is doubly difficult. I put a handkerchief around my wrist as a disruptive reminder. Forgetting remains a primary sin of the spiritual life. No, forgetting sounds too self-conscious. It is more a matter of reverting, unless one rewills the new in each moment. In time, perhaps, it will become natural. I intend to keep at it.

In reading a sheet of instructions given to me a bit late by the guest master, there was one point of interest—"One's cell is an area for complete silence." I would have assumed that it would be a natural place for a brief conversation if necessary. Br. "B" was useful—"The cell is sacred space, more holy even than the chapel. For it is there that you are utterly alone with God; it is for the two of you alone, and should not be compromised." Interesting indeed.

The place is a bit in a stir. Several dignitaries returned with the Abbot from his West Coast meeting. One is an eastern monk from Spencer, one a well-known scholar in monastic studies, and the third the Abbot General of the whole Cistercian system, based in Rome. So far they have kept me out of sight. My only impression of the Abbot General is that he has incredibly squeaky shoes. As for the monastic community, it is neither relaxed nor normal.

Sunday, June 18

The time is going too quickly—two and a half weeks here. The impression I have is that I am functioning more or less as a novice. At this level, there is little time that one would ordinarily call "time off." The work schedule is really six and a half days, with full liturgy seven days a week. The 2:45 rising is every day! Yet the amount of time available for prayer and reading is phenomenal; not counting liturgy time, I have available on an average day about seven hours.

I began today in earnest the companion prayer discipline. It is hard; I have to keep remembering and bringing myself back. The direction it is taking is using the analogy of a friend that I am showing around, as if s/he were a guest. This raises interesting theological issues—can God smell a lilac, enjoy the hot water of a shower, glory in seeing two eagles soaring low over the meadow? Yet I shared all of this in lively dialogue. It seemed almost sacrilegious at times, but I persevered. Total "familiarity" is perhaps only a first stage.

Couldn't hear any of the homily at Sunday Eucharist because of noisy infants. I understand why monks don't have children.

I am really on my own here. After putting chairs back after the morning liturgy I was free until 2:15. Still hungry for Scripture. After gathering eggs with Brother "H," I asked him about the time required to climb to the trailer hermitage on the high cliff overlooking the valley. He said an hour—I only had an hour before supper. I wanted to do it so badly that I climbed there, beyond, and back again in an hour. The view was glorious, the trailer hot and messy, and I—happy.

On return I found that the community was going to have a fun talk-time with the Abbot General over supper. So I was given a fast supper of toasted cheese sandwiches and helped to do a disappearing act. It was hard to sleep when I heard happy laughter in the background. Vivid childhood memories of painful rejection returned.

Monday, June 19

Three hours of early morning saturation in Scripture.

A strange day. At the eggery I was told to show Brother "G" how to do the job I have been doing. It is now, evidently, his job. Still sitting out of choir. Told to scrub unnecessary windows this afternoon. Every guest except me is included in everything, but then again they are all visiting monks. Strange feelings inside. Perhaps for the first time I am lonely. There is a vacancy. It really would not be very important whether I stayed or left.

Tuesday, June 20

At 4:20 A.M. a full moon floated along the south mountain and washed the night clean. I needed that. It was a night for completing my "typology" of prayer. I put in systematic form the definitions, types, methods that my research indicated have characterized spirit life through the centuries. I asked Fr. "E" to look at it when he can. This took four pages of outline. My final short summary, using terms somewhat arbitrarily but for sake of clarity, is this:

1. Prayer—literally means "to ask."
2. Meditation—reflection upon, for the sake of illumination.
3. Contemplation—delighting in, especially an object functioning as a sacramental.
4. Mysticism—ecstatic union with (sexuality providing a physical analogy).
5. Liturgy—conformity of external doing and interior consciousness in shaping rhythm which is pure art, i.e. for its own sake.
6. *Vocatio*—intermingling of daily doing and cosmic meaning—the intersections of time and eternity as commonplace.

A more traditional typology of prayer might be this.

I. Vocal—expressed audibly
  A. Private
  B. Public
II. Mental—expressed inwardly
  A. Diffused—intermingled with other activities
  B. Formal
    1. Discursive—logical, as in dialogue or meditation

2. Affective—intuitive/feeling
3. Contemplative
   A. Acquired (active)—openness through human effort
   B. Infused (passive)—union as divine gift

In secular life, much that keeps one going is anticipation—weekend, recreation, vacation. I have not found much of this here. One does look forward to a half day off Sunday, but really not to do something different. It provides more time to do what one does daily during the Vigil hours. The same is true of each monk's one week off for retreat. One could conclude from this that life is ideal when time off is concentration of rather than compensation for daily existence. What one looks forward to here is daily—especially the Vigil hours, and Eucharist.

The Old Testament is continuing to provide difficulty. This morning Solomon, the wisest of men, pleasing to God, acquired 700 wives, 300 prostitutes, and unbelievable affluence of palace and personal life. Even his ivory throne was covered with gold. If he averaged three intercourses per week, Solomon could see each of his official women friends once every ten years. Blessed be the name of the Lord!

I was permitted to attend a session with the Belgian scholar who is staying for a week. Very disappointing—I became so aware of the consuming subculture of the professional scholars, attending conferences to read papers to each other to satisfy the protocol of marking anniversaries of famous people and events, to war with minds over the minutiae of secondary matters. He told us about the books he had written, was writing, or would write, and how many papers he had been invited to read. I learned nothing. Rather sad.

In reading the Gospels, I am taken by how often Jesus used the phrase "Abba, Father." These words seem to distill his life of prayer, as companionship. Consequently, I have begun the discipline of "Abba evocation" as the ground for companion prayer. One repeats over and over again the name "Abba, Father." It is analogous to the way one learns to type—repeating

40

until it becomes second nature, never forgotten, so that even after a long absence one can nevertheless type immediately, but not without errors. To render indelible the name is to counter the plague of forgetting.

Wednesday, June 21

Brother "A" was bulldozing the top irrigation ditch and found a large hole that couldn't be filled. So this morning I helped install a large metal pipe. My task this afternoon was to dig out the water entrance on both sides of the pipe, and place rock to keep the earth from being eaten away. So at 2:30 I took the pickup, filled with rock, over pastures, through three gates, and finally up a very steep and scary "road" to the top. And there, utterly alone, snow hills all around, an eagle soared and finally perched on an evergreen beside me. I shoved and shaped the ground. In the warm sun I was ecstatic—swept by the wind—creating, with and for water. Epiphany. And I ate an orange!

In the evening we met again with the scholar. A bit better, but he still played hopscotch with ideas. I asked him, "If you were to create a monastery informed by the same intentionality as the first monasteries, where would you build it?" He replied, "The city."

Thursday, June 22

Received a letter from home, filled with the details and problems of house maintenance, car repairs, etc. It made me feel a little guilty that I was here, "running through the daisies," as the letter kidded. Yet I realize that what I am about is not only important but is also very difficult. It is no vacation. So I wrote immediately a six page letter trying to be as practical and helpful as possible, then sealed it, and returned more confidently to my own "work."

41

After lunch the Abbot asked if I would care to meet with him after work (4:30). We met in his office. His first statement set the caring context: "How are things with you, *really?*" He expressed his satisfaction that my integration into the community had occurred so well. "But," he asked, "do you really prefer not to sit in choir with the rest of us?" Surprised, I explained my lack of invitation, and he said he would speak with the guest master.

I related my feelings about prayer, that in coming to the monastery I felt the need to start all over again, as if I knew nothing. As a child, all I knew was petitionary prayer, and as my skeptical agnostic days occurred, I no longer believed in a God who would (could?) "manipulate the natural order" if you asked "him." So prayer simply faded out, without decision, without fanfare. I told him that often as the monks sat in silence in chapel, I longed to go up to each, peek into his eye to see if he was home, and then demand, *"What are you doing?"* My problem is not a lack of desire—it is fumbling over *what* to do. I explained, "I think the analogy of swimming applies." As a boy, I was just encouraged—you can do it. That wasn't helpful—I didn't know *what* to do. Then someone took the time to explain. But still I thrashed, barely staying up, going nowhere. I tried—but nothing, until one day, by chance, I seemed to relax—didn't do so much—and I took a stroke that was forward! That was all I needed. I had a "feel." And I knew, from then on, it was OK—the rest was a matter of practice. He heard me, with a warm laugh. His analogy was helpful. "It isn't as if you are trying to do what won't happen unless you do it—you may be trying too hard. You are already surrounded by God—you do not need to go to him, discover him, or do anything. Rather, let it be. Let yourself be addressed—it is God's doing, not yours." I described what I had been doing. He concurred at two points. First, the Abba repetition as an aid to remembrance. "Continue this, along with short prayers of request and thanksgiving before and after your daily activities. Ask for what you want." Second, he strongly recommended the reading of Scripture, especially because I desired it so much. He suggested that I read in order to grasp the whole, as I was doing; but in addition, after an hour or two, stop, think back over what I had read. "Center in on one passage, then maybe a sentence, and finally a word that speaks to you. Then in a special place, meditate on it." By meditate, he meant "resting in," "doing nothing," "being quiet," "sensing the presence of." His concern was that my readings on prayer were making the experiences of others a deterrence from my own praying. "They are only personal descriptions—you must do your thing in terms of what feels right for you." He seemed to regard my "enjoyment" of the silence, my "feeling good" about being alone but not lonely, as *actually* practicing the presence. Just letting be, not forcing, but resting, doing nothing, empty, wasteful. In reply to my feeling that I was really not praying, he replied, "You are surrounded already by a context of prayer—daily office, chanting, Eucharist. To be in that defining atmosphere is already to be 'doing it.' Let it soak in. Let it be."

We parted, late for supper, but with the idea that I would experiment for several days, and then "check in" periodically. I am very thankful. He is a kind, gentle person.

In the evening we met for the final time with Dom Jean Le-Clerq. He spoke of secularity having the positive effect of delimiting not only what certain doctrines mean (e.g. Trinity, Mary), but that for which prayer is appropriate and inappropriate. He gave the impression that much was up in the air for him, and that the idea of prayer as petititon smacked of magic.

I left with the feeling that theological rethinking forced upon him by the 1960's (a new "irreversible threshold signaled by walking on the moon, transistor communication, etc.") was, in its own way, what Protestantism has been going through for well over a century, and thus now with more precision. It isn't just a matter of relating psychology and theology. The issue is more precise—*what* psychology with *whose* theology? I said to him in the kitchen later what Barth long ago said to Bultmann— "You know too much," meaning that through science you claim to know what God can and can't do. Barth's alternative was: "Let God be God." If religion in general and Christianity in particular is what is left as science increasingly does its explanatory thing, then the process will continue as it began in Descartes: from external to internal, and then, with Freud, from the dead end of interiority into pluralistic subjectivity. If, for example, one rejects petitionary prayer (etymologically prayer means "asking"), not only does it cut at the heart of Scripture, but it undercuts fatally the image of "the God of history" (unless that symbol is reduced to the natural forces of evolution). It will not do to reduce prayer to self-forming, or, as Dom Jean suggested, "so to deal with myself that my aspirations are of the best," or even Morton Kelsey's proposal to use dreams to deal with portions of ourselves that are normally hidden from us. I am clear in my own mind that such approaches are for those who, for various reasons, "need" to be Christians, and are searching for ways to translate Christianity so that it can be more palatable. But I do not need to be a Christian. I find myself much more like an unbeliever who will believe only if it makes a significant difference. No longer is it honest to tell the non-believer that what he knows and experiences already is what we mean by "God" or "Christ" or "salvation" or "prayer." I will choose to name it by its simplest name, refusing to bootleg by capitalizing a word. One cannot experience love and claim God by writing it Love. "Relevance" and "insignificance" are the two edges of the religious dilemma.

Friday, June 23

On the way to Vigils, Fr. "F" whispered for me to leave my notebook in his box and he would look at my research about the types of prayer. I was delighted, having begun to wonder if silence might be affecting monastic memory.

Then a very strange thing happened—from 3:30 to 4:30 A.M. I'm not sure what to make of it. Over a cup of coffee in the refectory, I continued my reading of 2 Kings. As I read, passing from Elijah to his successor Elisha, the territory became weirdly familiar, although I had not read this section for over forty years. I read of the boys jeering Elisha, and accommodatingly he called the bears from the woods to eat them. Then I remembered. Every night before bed my mother had read to me "religiously" from Hurlbut's *Story of the Bible* (a literal treatment of the Bible stories, using much of the biblical material and dialogue itself). It all came flooding back. The God of the bears had been a frightening thing. But as I read, there was more—Elisha visited a couple who decided to build a "small roof chamber with walls, and put there a bed, a table, a chair and a lamp, so that whenever he comes to us, he can go in there." Very simple, of little consequence—yet I was overwhelmed. As a child, almost every night before going to sleep I would imagine building something with my hands, remodeling our house, much of which I actually came to do. Yet my favorite "fantasy" was a roof chamber. It was, as I now thought of it for the first time, monastic. I returned to my cell and, looking out over the hills, I knew I was in my roof chamber, the one I had wanted all my life.

I began reading again, and there was more. Elisha promised the woman a son, who as a boy died—an only child. I was that only child, the one who came to the fields saying. "Oh my head, my head!" I have had severe headaches for years, and had awakened with one this morning. He died. Elisha came and lay on him in that roof chamber, "his mouth upon his mouth, his eyes upon his eyes, his hands upon his hands, and as he stretched himself upon him the flesh of the child became warm." "Take up your son." For as far back as I can remember, I wanted to be a doctor—to raise up. I got as far as pre-medical school. I loved the work, but was turned off by the motivations of doctors. I became aware that "raising up" was of little value unless the life so raised was transformed. And so my pilgrimage, in ways I never planned or realized, took a religious turn. This is weird, but when I taught at Princeton, I joined an ambulance squad, learning first aid. The emergency call I most remember was to a child strangled in a tot's chair table. We used the resuscitator—everything we knew, rubbing him to make him warm. I failed, and finally, after an hour, I helplessly "took up" the boy, put him on a bed, covered him (refusing to cover his face), put his arms out over the blankets, as if asleep, and talked to him. A year later, mouth to mouth resuscitation was taught, and closed heart massage—I learned these with deep feeling—mouth to mouth, heart to heart.

But there is still more. Naaman was cured of leprosy by Elisha, who refused all reward. But his servant Gehazi ran after Naaman to receive silver and festive garments. My life has increasingly been involved in social change, against the obsession with silver, the doing for reward (I have a terrible time with the reward motif saturating the Gospel of Matthew) and the wearing of "festal garments."

There is more. The prophets living with Elisha said, "The place where we dwell under your charge is too small for us." And they built a log addition. All my life I have built additions—craved to build—I can think of at least three literal times. And only yesterday, in writing home, I was speaking of buying some land near water ("they went to the Jordan to get logs") and building, adding to the cabin as needed. Deep in my being is the need to build, to create, until God for me is the Creator, and the Gospel the call to cosmic co-creativity.

And as I pondered this flooding of memories and the placing of pieces, I remembered the name I had long ago secretly given myself—Ishmael: "Because the Lord has given heed to your affliction. He shall be a wild ass of a man, his hand against every man and every man's hand against him, and he shall dwell over against all his kinsmen." Now I saw Ishmael as the name of my craving—my being branded—different from—never resting in or with—why I came here! And this morning, as I reflected, it seemed that *Ishmael had become Elisha.* I do not know why—I do not know what it means.

Alone, in the chapel, the words came to me, "Taste and see that the Lord is good." They became transmuted in my mind to: "Savor the quietness in stillness." It was good.

Before Eucharist, I read on in 2 Kings and found a section that I could not recall. Enemy soldiers, coming to capture Elisha, were struck blind so that he led them into the capital of his own king. But instead of killing them, he said: "Set bread and water before them, that they may eat and drink and go to their master." And the bread and water became a "great feast." So in my own life, the daily essentials have increasingly become transformed into the feast which is the Eucharist—a new and central ingredient in my life.

This has been a rare morning. What does it all mean? I remember Bonhoeffer: One becomes a Christian when he first begins reading Scripture with the pronoun "we" and thus "I." It was I who passed unharmed through the Red Sea, yet in the desert made golden images. Somehow this morning I have had identified precisely this fact—I conceive the world, for better or worse, through eyes distinctly biblical, and the church as faith enculturation.

My wrestling was interrupted by the guest master who corrected me as to how to wash a plate, so as not to dirty the dish water.

Saturday, June 24

An idea from Kelsey during Vigils was helpful. Spirituality in the East is losing one's identity in the Cosmic consciousness; in the West, it is entering into relationship with the Cosmic Lover. This ties in well with Dom Jean's observation that Bernard of Clairvaux insisted upon the body as essential in knowing God. Even in the life to be, Christian faith talks of a bodily existence. Dom Jean's explanation of St. John of the Cross' insistence that the final entrapments to be negated are temporality, sensuality, and affection is that it is only in negating them entirely that they are given back sevenfold. Perhaps this is what Ezekiel means by the new "heart of flesh" (11:19).

Through the day I became more and more aware of the appropriateness of sexuality as analogies for the life of spirit. Teresa of Avila freely speaks of it in terms of marriage and ecstatic union, and Bernini's statue portrays her in a trance as if in the throes of orgasm. It is no wonder that some religions have practiced worship through the sexual act—the loss of self in other, in which time and space melt into the ecstatic now. Nor is it any wonder that sex in our culture is a substitute for God, and an unacknowledged surrogate prayer life. But it is a foretaste that in satisfying produces more profound longing. Such thinking ties in well with the final section by Nouwen read in Vespers. The crucial importance of the empty center in our being in an age of self-realization is symbolized by celibacy. Sexual absti- nence is not the negation of sexuality but its spiritualization as divine longing, and for some, evidently, Divine-human consum- mation. I yearn for this, but it does not seem to be for me—yet I understand. Using the same analogy, the clue to life in the spirit is simplicity—to will one thing—a kind of monogamy of being, a faithful lover.

I had a session with Fr. "E" about the prayer typology I gave him to read. He called it "beautiful," especially underscor- ing the idea of God enjoying his creation through us. He quoted Gandhi as saying that the cosmos is the garment of God—reject it and one receives it back as a gift. Two other insights he had. He put it well by characterizing the mantra as giving the mind a plaything to keep it quiet so that we can be centered about more important things, namely, the presence of God. I asked him if he had ever experienced God clearly. He thought, and re- plied, "Not in such a way that it can't be doubted." He went on to talk about his experiences, mostly with nature and particular- ly with the mountains. Despite his interest in Eastern thought, he insisted upon this world and the self as realities not to be re- jected. "But," he concluded, "there are key experiences in which I am so absorbed that nothing exists but the experience. If East- ern thinkers are describing not the nature of life as unity but the nature of such experience then I know what Nirvana is."

This morning Br. "B" and I had a real adventure. Strapping equipment on a motorcycle, we started off across the mesa to fix fences where a four wheeler can't go. After spilling in several irrigation ditches, we finally made it, incredibly muddy but strangely happy. The afternoon was harder but equally meaningful. After several invitations, Brother "A" and I agreed to try our hand at resodding barren parts of the garth. We worked hard for two hours and only had a patch six feet by two eked out against "one great wilderness." But it was enough with which to experiment before we tried any more.

During the hours of work I sensed in my companion an unwillingness to share any negativity regarding the community or any person. In secular life such denial, negation, or internalization would be psychologically undesirable. The only positive way for me to see this process is that such inevitable feelings are being dealt with honestly and straightforwardly in the life of dialogue with God. I do not know if this is occurring. I am uneasy.

Sunday, June 25

I looked forward to Sunday Eucharist. The homily was preached by a visiting monk. It is necessary, he said, for Christians to have courage to stand up to political leaders. So far, so good. "Of course there is little necessity for this in the West, but in Communist countries . . ." Oops. I felt angry, hurt, betrayed. Similarly, in a conversation with Dom Jean yesterday about the U.S., I commented on the fear I see in people today. Before I could say more, he interrupted: "Yes, I know. I'm close to East Germany and you never know when those Communists might do anything." How powerfully emerges the image of the speck in the neighbor's eye and the log in one's own. I am deeply concerned: spirit life as refuge, and as support for the status quo. This monastery is loved by the wealth of Aspen. During our morning prayers I felt the need to pray for Solzhenitsyn: "When he judged the Soviet Union we listened and applauded; when he turns his propheticism toward us and our country, we are quick to judge." In a speech at Harvard he identified Americans as a greedy lot, serving as no model. "Russia," he said, "has now achieved a spiritual development of such intensity that the

Western system in its present state of spiritual exhaustion does not look attractive.... A fact that cannot be disputed is the weakening of human beings in the West while in the East they are becoming firmer and stronger." Carl Rowan quoted Khrushchev who in 1959 said much the same: "The spirit of individualism, personal gain, greed for profits, hostility and confusion—such is the essence of bourgeois morality. The exploitation of man by man on which bourgeois society is built, represents the grossest violation of morals."

I had hoped that in this total monastic dedication to God alone, the basis for propheticism would emerge, and with it a new social option.

The bulletin board indicated that we are having a picnic with Brother "G"'s parents. After lunch, the guest master called me outside and said that I was "free tonight to determine my own schedule." Translated, this meant, "You are not invited." Feelings surfaced in me that go back to childhood. It seems that fear at its heart is response to the possibility of being left; and anger at its heart is the response to rejection. As the monks drove down the road, I turned toward the aspen forest. As I meditated, I realized that rejection is not an exception in life but the rule. Death is the final and total rejection; other times are token reminders of the final one. Thus my anger is misplaced. Somehow spirit life begins in the courage to stand alone, to expect nothing more, and strangely to glory in it. The unspoken premise seems to be "If God be for us ..." But that depends on Death being God's foe as well. Perhaps I have things turned around. Doing in order to belong, to find favor: that is to function as one does in the secular world, and it is backward. I am here on my own pilgrimage, and each monk is on his own. True. And yet—am I to begin with anger over political naiveté, in order to end up with advocating spiritual free enterprise?

As I walked the forest in its primitive silence, I detected why it is so crucial for spirit life. It is the empirical side of emptiness, as darkness is the empirical side of aloneness—without them the craving is assuaged. Hopefully there will also be psychic silence—the silence of the noisy city. At least may I never forget the Trappist dictum: "Speak only when it improves the silence."

When I returned I had the monastery to myself. So in the huge refectory I turned up at full power Beethoven's Eighth Symphony, cooked up the biggest batch possible of the "forbidden" french fries, and, somewhat smugly, watched the sun go down.

Monday, June 26

This was an "image" day—insights, pictures, hints. A phrase came during the reading of Ezra 4: "the Province Beyond the River." The text even capitalizes it. This is the context: "This city is a rebellious city, hurtful to kings and provinces, and that sedition was stirred up in it from of old. That was why this city was laid waste. We make known to the King that, if this city is rebuilt and its walls finished, you will then have no possession in the Province Beyond the River." In a sense, a monastery (as parable of the church) should be such a Province—no longer under the control of any political structure. By its purity as a faithful alternative, it would be the source of sedition to any system not grounded on community as known in foretaste in the Eucharist (the unconditional breaking and distributing of bread).

Recently I find myself spontaneously giving what I would lightheartedly call a "cosmic chuckle." I remember particularly when I looked out at the dawn—incredible pink-yellow clouds adorning the head of "Silver Mountain." I laughed, from way down deep. It is beyond grasp—you can't do anything with it. In being overwhelmed. what else can you do but chuckle? The laugh of creation at herself, it would seem, in sheer delight.

How that contrasts with the howling, yelping, wailing cries of the coyotes before dawn—I would like to believe it is a love song to the moon, but that is for romantics who have never heard them. They are more like the wail of the earth's oppressed—they are almost the craving turned terrifying. Just as they began, I was reading Job (23:8–9):

> Behold, I go forward, but he is not there;
> and backward but I cannot perceive him;
> on the left hand I seek him, but I cannot behold him;
> I turn to the right hand, but I cannot see him.

Am I forever to be limited to God as the postulate of my craving, without which the insatiability is the echo of an insane universe that stirs up that which taunts in its non-existence? Dorothee Soelle once wrote that Freud was right in identifying religion as endless wishing. But does it follow that "Blessed are the homesick for they shall come home"?

A letter from a friend spoke of Wesley—"living out his conviction/faith for years before 'the strange warming of his heart' occurred. What patience that took to keep on keeping on, without the more obvious signs—it sounds as if you have longed for the 'signs' and the experience for a long time and that your putting yourself where you are at this time is most significant." Perhaps.

Walking down the morning road to work a phrase from somewhere deep down emerged—"the hermit of the heart," or perhaps, the "hermit heart." The courageous aloneness of the long distance runner—aloneness, not loneliness. I was at a symphony once with friends—during the intermission I noticed a woman by herself, sitting with a motorcycle helmet on her lap. Instant admiration. The courage to be alone. I saw her afterward as she mounted the cycle and drove away in the rain. It is a gift, a rare gift, to be happy, utterly alone. And since we all are alone really, what does that say about how many of us are truly happy? The power of the hermit heart—a gift, surely. I would have it.

During a prayer session in the morning I let my mind roam peacefully—nice.

This was another day of "promotion." At the eggery I was

trained as a packer—using the twelve socket vacuum lifter for taking eggs from the sorting conveyers to the appropriate cartons. I did rather well, give or take a few eggs. On returning I was awarded a seat in choir, beside the novice, furthest from the Abbot. It had a comfortable feel, of joining the family.

After supper, I learned again, as I keep forgetting, the purging, calming, purifying presence of nature. I opened the door and walked out into the evening—two steps was all it took. Peace.

Tuesday, June 27

I am into Ecclesiastes now—one of my soberingly favorite books. Two passages emerged as the center for meditation:

> He has made everything beautiful in its time; also
> he has put eternity into man's mind, yet
> so that he cannot find out what God has done
> from the beginning to the end (3:11).

> Better is a handful of quietness
> than two hands full of toil and a striving
> after wind (4:6).

Somehow the two seemed to be a deeply connected summary for me.

I am interested in the variety of early morning responses. Some monks stay in the chapel for periods of meditation; some head directly for the kitchen (none, however, arrive at the coffee pot as quickly as I). Some go jogging at dawn; I wonder if any of them ever sneak back to bed.

Today I tried to summarize the key meanings that seem to be emerging for me thus far.

1. The need for discipline, beginning with the Abba repetition, serving as a remembrance of companion presence as basis for the new consciousness process. In time I must exercise more

the practice of seeing others, in fact everything, from that consciousness, i.e., under promise.

2. The Eucharist as the deeply moving center. It is foretaste and expectancy, sealed not yet with the subjectivity of personal sign (which I desire), but grounded importantly in the objective, believing community as foundation.

Something very interesting happened around noon. Almost ten minutes before lunch black clouds began rolling quickly —up one side of the mountains and sloshing down the other. The sun went out. As we ate in what was to be silence, the noise circling the monastery was enormous—whining, whistling, gusting, shaking. It occurred to me that if the belfry goes, hibernation under the oak tables is for me. Even though we are trained here never to seek out a person's eyes, we all looked up from our plates, giving each other kind of "wow" glances. Now the point. Being saturated for weeks in the theological world of the Old Testament, I know what should have occurred to us: What have we done wrong? Which of us has sinned? Why is God doing this to the valley? But never once did it enter our minds. What does this mean then if Scripture is filled with the law of reward and punishment, with the Lord of history who visits penalties of nature on those who are unfaithful, and yet this is no longer even a dim pattern in our thinking? When does accommodation or compromising or modernizing come to constitute substitution? This relates directly to prayer. Prayer means petition—but if one no longer believes in a God who operates in ways other than natural law, how much of biblical faith is left?

Last night I dreamed that I was to die soon. So I chose this to be the day. The feel was one of eerie, profound sadness—of looking at people and mountains and flowers for the last time. Whatever else the dream means, too much of our lives is spent in justifying ourselves competitively—books, articles, or lament over each—until a point is reached when none of it matters. The moment of "too late," and any justification that one has tentatively acquired, is negated anyhow—living between the "not yet" and the "too late to live."

The wild "sod" we transplanted continues to look even sadder than yesterday, with a kind of placid, indifferent and defiant yellow.

Wednesday, June 28

This is a day for which I have been waiting for a long time. I have no way of knowing if it will last, or what if any will be its implications. I simply know that in a deep sense this day was an answer. It started before daybreak. I was reflecting upon some letters that I had to write to three friends who want not to be excluded from what is happening to me. But in one sense nothing is happening. I can tell them about chickens, the toilets I scrub, the sunsets I watch. I feel like a monk at the still point of a turning wheel—moving but unmoved. For them it may be serenity; for me it has a feel of suspension. I really had nothing to write.

At Lauds I decided, all of a sudden, to claim my ordination. During intercessions acknowledgment is often made of anniversaries, as when Dom Jean had said, "Help me to pray to the Lord for perseverance to continue on, on this the 49th anniversary of my entering the monastery." In all truth I did not know the exact day of my ordination and had to do a quick mental calculation to ascertain the year. Yet it seemed unexplainably right to give thanks for this the 24th anniversary of my ordination on this the Feast Day of Irenaeus, my dear theologian friend from whom I have learned so much. I had never really claimed it before. But now I did, in the firm awareness of its central meaning: celebration of the Eucharist. And as I gave the prayer, I suddenly saw that it stood at the precise midpoint of my life thus far. The celebrant closed the intercessions with the passing of the peace, and three brothers (very dear to me) embraced me, for the first time, with the press of cheek to cheek.

At the moment of Communion, I gave the private prayer that I had given a hundred times in the past weeks: "Lord, show me a sign, that somehow I may experience your presence, no longer as hope but as fact." I am sure the request is in part triggered by the Old Testament expectation of signs from God. But it is far more. Liturgy, practice, prayer discipline—all of these I can do and find meaningful, but there is a hollow center, for they do not rest on a "givenness" of experience, on the basis of which one builds in risk. Nevertheless, I asked, having unconsciously concluded that such experience is not for me.

As I communed, in the midst of the petition I felt myself internally *released* to pray. Words tumbled silently out—biblical, liturgical words and names and phrases: "Thou who hast the world in your hand, who in this moment hast come as companion, I thank you without adequate praise to tell you—thank you for ..." And words flowed—friends, mountains, Christ, streams, cities, mistakes, craving, on and on. But most important, I knew this to be the "sign." Nothing huge, nothing shattering. Just a quiet knowing beyond knowledge that *I was on the other side.* No "if," or "perhaps," or "how." I was doing it; no, it was being done. The blockage, the resistance, the scars of false and sentimental and possessive and folksy piety, it no longer mattered. In fact, some of that very language flowed with a smile on my face. "Praise the Lord." It's okay, as long as I keep chuckling.

And as I drank from the cup I remembered vividly an event in 1953—my second year of seminary. I was at Yale, not to become a minister, not to affirm Christianity. I was exploring philosophically and theologically the question of meaning. That year, largely through scriptural studies, I came to the conclusion that without the resurrection there would be no Gospel—period. Clear. Historically unmistakable. And so was logic. Since I did not believe that the resurrection was fact, there was no Gospel for me. Continued residence at a seminary was meaningless. I gave myself one month to live with that awareness, before moving on. There was no alarm, no shock. It just was so. This did not reduce my energy for study and exploration; if anything it intensified it. Then one morning, as I awoke—I remember it clearly: the sun unusually brilliant, casting shadows through the leaves onto the bed—I found that I was operating from the "other side." I don't know how else to put it. Before then, any theological statement I made operated from an implicit conditional—"if." Now it had quietly moved to a "because," or "since." Theology was now a matter of working from and living out the implications. Put another way, I was now strangely operating from within rather than without. Not that I knew what the resurrection meant in any clear fashion—the difference was that "facticity" no longer was at primary issue.

All of this returned to me in a flash. And now this moment seemed to be stage two, as it were, of being on the other side. Conversation, dialogue, thanksgiving, companionship—these were now natural, "permitted"—no longer an "if" situation. I do not want to read too much into it; neither do I wish to discount it. With joy, I let it be.

When I finished my work early, I volunteered to help Br. "C" in the kitchen. He is a gracious, kindly, simple person with a finely honed sense of humor, but he tends to disclaim his ability with phrases like "Although I'm not learned ..." or "Although I'm only a brother among you priests ..." He did not know my background. So I told him: I am very educated and very ordained—and you have what I do not have and what you can give me. He seemed almost physically stopped by this. I told him that I knew much but had practiced little. While I was only beginning to pray, it was a way of life for him, born of years of monastic discipline. He believed me and opened up in a new way. He resembled Br. Lawrence, practicing the presence among his pots and pans. Somewhere between the cauliflower and the squash, prayer became defined as experiencing God as he who knows all of my weirdness and weaknesses, and loves me anyhow; and our rejoicing together in that acceptance. "Prayer," he explained, "is sitting still with a word or phrase and getting lost in it." "Like at Mass, the words, 'This is my body.' I rarely get much help by reading about other people praying—I have to do it. I just talk with him. Any time is important, like now—we need to tell him how overwhelmed we are by these squash—look at the shade of yellow—and you can eat them. Wonder if God ever ate a squash. What a shame to make them and not taste them."

Then he made his offering. "I'm not going to tell you who did it, but I heard a tape that really says it the way I know it, and I spent days writing the important things in a notebook. I study it; haven't really gotten past the first page—I consider each word. If you want, I'll let you read it." By afternoon the notebook was in my mail box. His favorite passages he marked in yellow. His kindness reminded me of one other thing he said, in disagreeing with some of the readings at lunch. "Blacks and women too need all the breaks we can give them—that they can take. What else does it means to be a Christian?"

It rained in the afternoon—a quiet gentle enfolding rain— our first really. I particularly experienced two verses from the Vespers' psalms: "God is my possession forever" (72); "I will thank the Lord with all my heart . . ." (110).

Later as I prepared for bed, the mountain emerged from the mist as its garland; when I closed my drapes it was as if God were having fun. Like a painter in final delight, he put a dab of cloud at the very peak.

Thursday, June 29

After yesterday, it would seem that there should be no more. I remember how cheated I felt by one of my favorite novels, G. Bernanos' *Diary of a Country Priest*. At the moment of breakthrough, with the words, "Does it matter? All is grace," the priest dies. That's cheating. Moses was majestic until he came down from the mountain and blew the whole scene in anger. *How do you live it, knowing it will fade, that doubt will eat at it, that it's unclear, and that the examples are either embarrassing or few?* All that I can hope for, I think, is like Faulkner's epiphany at the death of Joe Christmas in *Light in August:* that it will always be there, unthreatening, often unobserved, but indelibly there no matter at what fireside or what daily closing. So be it.

In cleaning I found a pamphlet entitled "Celebration of the Death of a Cistercian." It described the whole process from the tolling of the bells as the death of a monk approaches (that all may gather around him in prayer and none may die alone) to the final procession for the Commemoration of all the Faithful Departed. There came over me a deep and profound sadness—not fear, but sadness. I thought of some of my friends, racked with the final agony of leukemia, who needed desperately to die, but even then found it hard to "let go." Analogies flooded me, of letting go into death. To have life taken from you—yes. But this was new, like climbing to the top of a high sliding board, knowing that having come this far you will go down, but sitting there, holding on, waiting for the courage. To let go, not simply of *my* life but of life itself—of creation, of the only home I have ever not had. I was reminded of Barth, who said that the only ones capable of understanding the good news of the Resurrection are those deeply in love with the earth. I don't know when I have felt such sadness. I went to the chapel, and prayer tumbled out as it had the day before. It was an Emmaus-like prayer. With the Presence, my spirit "brooded over the waters" of my past. The thread of meaning—the cry for companionship, the fear of being left—all the craving which until now was not known for what it was. "Their eyes were opened." I remember feeling the words—you are in this deep—beyond the point of recall. There came a quiet peace—but nothing taken away. A kind of OKness born of wisdom. The morning sun was beginning to test the overcast sky. I rested on my bed for a while—it was all too much.

I progressed as a full-time worker in the eggery. It was good to hold my own with the "pros"—it is fast, "assembly line" production. The eggs keep on coming, they set the pace, and if an egg breaks, ha! Could be the place for knowing panic, but all was at peace. It felt good to work long, hard, productively.

In the evening there was a community meeting without me.

I did not have to be told. I knew, and was delighted that it did not bother me. I picked up my mail—three letters from friends, each one sadder than the one before. I felt a bit overwhelmed, lonely, helpless, sad. It was like the messengers coming to Job. I was on the verge of guilt. One said, "I long for the kind of support that you are feeling with the brothers." Another, from a person who had known me for over twenty years, was cause for thought. Reflecting on a rationale for me, of all people, being in a monastery, she guessed: You must be "plotting revolution." The third letter seemed to be a conclusion, posed both as exclamation and as question: "The dichotomy of your being is a phenomenon!?" I remembered Hesse's confession: I have always been a seeker, like the lives of all who have given up trying to deceive themselves—it is a mixture of nonsense and chaos, madness and dreams.

As I called it a day, I tried to be appreciative that my "breakthrough" had not long been permitted to go untested and unthreatened. The agony of relating the life of spirit and the agony of the world: silence and crying, community and oppression, Abba and the satanic, monastery and the inner city. I opted for listening to the gentle rain.

Friday, June 30

This is hard to believe, but it is a good touch. Yesterday, as I was energetically packing eggs, a small blonde, blue-eyed child from a neighboring ranch wandered in. "Hi," I said, "What's your name?" With a huge grin came the reply, "Elisha!"

I had an interesting conversation with a visiting monk concerning two primary changes in the Trappists since he entered in 1960. (1) The shift from Latin, Gregorian liturgy to modern forms. "We were regarded as the second best monastery for Gregorian chanting in the whole order. Suddenly our status became a symbol of conservatism." The important result, however, is that "now we attend liturgy more out of joy than duty."

(2) The evolution from cenobitic practice to something closer to Carthusian. Formerly we were totally silent hermits in community. Everything was together; we even slept together in a huge semi-partitioned dormitory, forbidden to be alone in our "cell" during the day. Everyone was almost always visually related. Now we have moved into individual rooms which are real "cells." In these much of our sacred time is spent, never to be entered or invaded by others. "This is to be both genuinely eremitic and now verbally communal. It is new."

The Abbot invited me to visit. I chose to read three key sections from my journal to bring him into my journey. He nodded throughout in approval, and "blessed" what had been occurring. His concern was that I be able to let go of such experiences, without clutching on or trying to recreate them. Otherwise I will be tempted to structure for myself where the spirit may lead. A crucial difference between secular and monastic life rests in the contrast between a lifestyle of "doing to" versus "letting be." "Be willing to be led," he concluded, "wherever that goes." He suggested that, instead of lengthening the fifteen minutes of morning prayer, I try another fifteen minutes before supper, again centering it around Scripture. He thought that in a week or so I would be ready to concentrate on "centering prayer," which is already beginning.

At a communal supper, Br. "I" (the hermit) and I had an excellent conversation. He has been looking for years, undecided between being a hermit on his own versus in a monastic context. We shared the difficulties of creating alone space and alone economic support today. He concluded that the offer made by this monastery to him could not be matched—to build a hermitage wherever he wants, and to check in a year to see how the arrangement is working. Our conversation seemed to provide confirmation and perspective that was helpful. Around September 1, several of his hermit-type friends are coming; "We will camp together in Schoefield Pass. Please come with us." "I must leave September 1." "If they can't make it earlier, then maybe you and I can do it—I'd like that." "We'll see."

I went outside after Vespers. The rain had stopped, and a slanted sun was slyly emerging. And the "sod" we planted was green, for the first time.

Saturday, July 1

While repairing fences with the novice, I found that it was almost impossible for him to understand the agony of my struggle. For him the non-existence of God is not even entertainable. The struggles with which I identify would be for him pre-Christian, perhaps even un-Christian. He has read about aridity of spirit being almost inevitable, but he has not known this. He fears it. It seemed impossible to tell him what is happening to me without it seeming to be a confession of faithlessness, or a breakthrough into the obvious. Neither sounds right.

In a letter to a secular friend who is going through a crisis, I wrote of the pilgrimage that all of us are on: "For a depth that sufficiently grounds the heart of a 'hermit' to stand strong, to be solitary without being undone by loneliness. To be able to feel in the midst of Kansas City or Laramie what one senses standing on Capital Peak. Whether embraced by sun, or threatened by clouds, to know it is OK both ways. Perhaps a wisdom regarding inevitabilities, a sense of 'being ledness,' to go and pursue and risk where you 'have' to go and do and be. Maybe the word 'faithful' sounds right—not necessarily to anyone but to life, to the land, perhaps, to oneself." This, of course, is third-rate babbling. It makes sense at 2:45 A.M. in the darkness.

Sunday, July 2

I am sensing an interesting shift in me. It is July now; my stay is one-third over. Before this week I was counting the days, backward as it were, wanting time to stop. Now it is OK. It is as if a foundation is being built, and while I am pleased to be here, I will be ready to go.

It was a beautiful day, so I decided to sit in the sun and concentrate on Scripture. I was more than ready to finish the Old Testament. I was taken by *how* different the Old Testament and Paul feel—especially on such matters as reward or punishment for a "perfect life," versus the graciousness of God. It is important that I remember, however, the degree to which the final two redactions to the Old Testament were the Priestly and Deuteronomic editors, giving to the whole their own theological flavor. As I reflected on the essential impact of the Old Testament as a whole, I named for myself ten characteristics:

1. Covenant—with exodus the gracious act on which all else depends.
2. Promised land—the ideal community of justice—its claim demands faithful response—it gives rise to a universal vision.
3. Obedience/reward; sin/judgment (personal, communal, national).
4. Sacrifice in the Jerusalem temple as central—rightly done.
5. Law, requiring total obedience in all things.
6. Justice—e.g. for the sojourner, for once we were sojourners.
7. Lord of history—increasing identity of the Creator and the God of history.
8. Direct revelation through both priest and prophet.
9. Increasing pessimism over human performance.
10. Anger of God mellowing in time with dimensions of compassion.

Sunday is our music day at lunch, but I was not prepared for Roger Williams! The center of our liturgical meal, it would seem, was: "I Left My Heart in San Francisco."

I called home for the first time since being here. It was hard, re-entering another world, with the joy of relating to it and them. Perhaps the most interesting comment was the response to my description of what had happened last Wednesday. After patient hearing of my "breakthrough" came these words:

"Beautiful. It is that kind of experience that makes monastics kind and naive. They mistake sheltered environment for the whole world, and when they come out they get hurt and awakened. Yet it is an experience necessary for surviving in the inner city, making it necessary to leave from time to time to rediscover it. The hardest of your tasks is to relate the two worlds."

The last thing I heard as I was hanging up was a police siren. I walked out into the twilight; the sounds here were of birds, cattle, and a playful ground squirrel.

Monday, July 3

Perhaps the importance of this day is that I completed the whole Bible. Just before Eucharist, I read the final Amen. It has been a significant experience, for which the final Book of Revelation is a soaring crescendo—only Handel has come close to a fitting response. It is not to be analyzed and "understood," but choreographed and read poetically to music. The vision of a final consummation of creation, hinted as possibility when first the spirit brooded over the primal waters; history became the plane of creativity, as God so shaped the work of his hands that the characters themselves came alive, resisting the playwright, inducing God no longer to be the sabbatical enjoyer but the tragic incarnate craftsperson, as together the dream is lost and found and reconstituted. There will be that point when all may look back from the peak and for the first time know that they would not have had it otherwise. Then and only then can there be a *Te Deum* by sound rather than fragile hope.

This is the Fourth of July weekend. I am glad that there seems to be no intention here to observe it. In my final biblical reading, it was difficult not to find analogy with the United States: "The merchants of the earth have grown rich with the wealth of her wantonness. . . . Come out of her, my people, lest you take part in her sins" (Rv. 18). To be rigorously monotheistic and monastically intentional about a life style totally faithful is to be a radical, if not a revolutionary.

In my beginning thoughts on survival Christianity in the city, I remembered Bonhoeffer's "secret discipline"—a piety of the closet, of the inner sources, of the incarnate life style—in but not of, involved but not fed by, free in the midst of, free from in order to be free for the spiritually unknown. It is to take seriously Bultmann's owning "as if not." Or Kierkegaard's Knight of Faith, who enjoys all of common life, indistinguishable from others except that he marches internally to a different drummer. Merton speaks of the spiritual underground, declaring that detachment is not from things and others but from ourselves; thereby one gains a new perspective for seeing and using all things in and for God. The obstacle to seeing no evil in anything created by God is our own egotistic self.

It is strange that one as involved in the life of spirit as I should be is so turned off by "religious" things. Recently in going through a city I saw a sign: "Jesus Park." I cringed. The quest for spirit life must in many ways be a secret pilgrimage of inner transformation that makes all things new, but frees us not to be different from but to be involved with, in liberated ways. We do not become "religious"—we become free and thus faithful.

It has taken a long time, but now I know that there are three kinds of bell ringing here. The first is ten solitary rings, which is the call to an office. Second is the regular ringing, indicating the beginning of the office itself. The third is the ringing three times a day of the Angelus, a call to remembrance. It consists of three individual sounds, three different times, followed by regular ringing. It occurs morning, noon, and the last thing at night. I discovered this when the bell rang, calling us, I thought, to lunch. I barreled out of the library, only to see Fr. "E" standing motionless. Going right by, I spotted the Abbot ahead, likewise occupied. Not thinking the odds promising that both would be watching ants simultaneously, I too stopped and watched mythical ants until the bells stopped. Later I asked questions.

At the eggery we pack with a vacuum lifter that holds a dozen eggs at a time, to be released by pressing a button, preferably into a carton. I had done fine, but today I was given a new lifter that holds thirty eggs at a time. I lifted three times successfully. Then on the fourth time suddenly thirty eggs, for reasons still unknown, crashed to the machinery and were converted into instant omelets. For the rest of the morning my ability was hampered—each lift was with anxiety, lacking both trust and confidence. And every insignifcant noise sounded like the eschatological harbinger of the great egg demise. As I thought of this paralysis of effective action, I thought of how each of us needs the healing of memories. It does not take many failures, rejections, losses, putdowns, until the memory is wounded. A black and blue memory becomes the filter for narrow and tentative imaginations on the present, blinding us to the future. The Spirit must cure such remembrance through a reconstituting acceptance which is nothing less than essential memory displacement. Soelle once said that ego power depends upon the closeness of God—the awareness that one is not forsaken or abandoned.

In the evening during another closed community meeting, visiting Fr. "F" and I had a conversation in the washroom. In noting that for two straight nights the community meetings had made Vespers too late for us to wait, we commented that things seem to have an "ominous" quality. Just as I turned off my light and was settling down in bed, the bell for Vespers finally rang. It was a rare experience to fall asleep to the quiet chanting of the evening office—rare indeed.

Tuesday, July 4

I was wrong. This was the Fourth of July and it was acknowledged. Surprisingly, however, the intercessions at Lauds were solid: "We thank you that this country was begun with the right to life, liberty, and the pursuit of happiness; forgive us for the narrowness of this conception and strengthen us that this revised meaning may be universalized to all." The "worst" was a prayer for the oppressed in the Soviet Union, in Africa and in

South America, leaving unrecognized the oppressed in our own nation.

I finished my work early enough to help in picnic preparations. It was exciting. Pizza pies that violated wholeheartedly the laws of the diet, mountains of salad, beer, three kinds of wine, and all the home-made ice cream and fresh strawberries you could eat. Everyone was open, relaxed, laughing—it was mellow, caring. I realize how rare it is for men to be so gentle in enjoying each other. Br. "I" has been working for two years, with certain disasters, to complete the digging of a mile-long water line, six feet deep, to the guest house. He is getting within sight of the end. But in the midst of the party he came in slowly. One of the irrigation ditches had somehow been diverted, filling his whole trench so that the sides were falling in. A beer was put in each of his pockets, and he was sent out stoically to face the world again, promising that he would come back soon, no matter what. "We're in it together." This is a small monastery, and they really do not have enough people to do the work—but they deserve to survive. They really do.

In the evening Fr. "F" showed slides of the dedication of the new Trappist chapel at Spencer. Many of the monks here were originally from Spencer. For them it was like old home week, seeing pictures of old friends and new beards. It was mixed. Comments of sadness: "He left us last year," "Brother Bill is married now," "All three of these left about the same time." And yet, the fun just of being together, especially with seconds on ice cream and strawberries. After washing dishes we were so tired that we just remained at a table in the refectory for shortened Vespers, and decided to sleep in late (3:30 A.M.)! It was a mellow evening. I was very happy.

Wednesday, July 5

It was with eagerness that I spent the early morning hours working on an idea that has been emerging throughout my time here. There are so many approaches to spirit life, often competitive, reflected by such judgments as "superficial" and "mature," "preliminary" and "advanced" stages. While there is no doubt some progression possible in spirit life, an analogy from art seems useful. Must we decide between Cézanne and Van Gogh? Are they not two contrasting and yet legitimate ways of perceiving reality? I began to link this idea of spiritual pluralism with the image of God as Triune. There is a rich pluralism *within* God (Father, Son, and Spirit), as well as in God's relation to the world (Creator, Redeemer, Inspirer). A one-to-one identification of these two types of images is inadequate because it does not involve all of God in each function. But if we see each "Person" involved in each "function," our imagination gains a richness of at least nine dimensions to spirit life. For example, the "Father" as Creator points toward the unfathomable abyss of creativity at the depth of all things, experienced as mystery. Eastern spirituality particularly is characterized by this losing of oneself in the pregnant nothingness. We sense this as the ominous innateness of energy in the paintings of Nolde, or the shimmering formlessness of a Monet. Likewise, the "Son" or Logos also is Creator, but characterized here by the intentional form in all things—the structure, the shape and contours invading reality with purposiveness. One delights in this mode of spirituality through the elementary forms of a Cézanne, or even the pure formal abstraction of a Mondrian. And the Spirit too is Creator, sensed as the restless, surging driving *élan vital* of immanental process, as in the paintings of Van Gogh, Vlaminck, and Jackson-Pollack. These are only three of the possible dimensions that are necessary to reality, but yet by focus each takes on a uniqueness as the other modes of spirit life fade to the background. It is exciting to sense the richness of life lived in the relational Presence of an incredibly rich Deity.

The "ominous" feel in the monastery lately, and the closed meetings, are becoming clear. Rumor was substantiated when Br. "A" began assuming Br. "D's" tasks, including supervision of me. Therefore . . . Br. "D" is leaving. It is like an unacknowledged death in the family.

I had fun this afternoon riding the grass mower. The grass

around the monastery had grown knee deep. If I have a few more tries at it we may have the biggest golf course (without holes) west of the Mississippi. I forgot the ground squirrels—we have plenty of holes.

Thursday, July 6

I am increasingly aware of the appropriateness of sexual analogies for spiritual life. The mystic language is one of unity, interpenetration, ecstasy, love, loss in the other, flight, fantasy, wedding, union. Listen to St. John of the Cross' phrases: "For sick with love I am." "Save only if of thee I have my fill." "Now blooms our nuptial bed." "Of my beloved drank I deep indeed." "Love her sole delight." "Wounded by my glance that on thee played." An article of mine will be published soon exploring Mary and God (as successor for Israel and Yahweh) as parable distilling the Divine-human relation as love affair. It is no wonder that so many religions have developed from the sexual archetype, but often restricted to the fertility dimension. One can tie this to a Freudian understanding of sexual periods. The first is the need for that supportive, enfolding grounding which provides foundation for all that follows. Then after a period of independence ("I'll do it myself"), there is the second wave (puberty) as a bewildering reaching out. In the craving to belong, independence is seared by the need for the "other." There seem to be later periods as well, in which after early adult competitiveness even the most assured of us are forced to reach beyond. Such a broad and deep "sexual" reaching is the physical aspect of what theologically Tillich has identified as craving the metaphysical "reunion of the separated." This is the spiritual quest, as longing and as paradigm.

Is it too much to say then that I fell in love today? We had our Thursday night Eucharist—gentle, quiet, together, warm, enfolding. After the cruciformed blessing we flowed out. As I reached the window of the far cloister, there in the yard was an incredibly beautiful doe: gentle, quiet. As each monk came out, we gathered at the window—the "gesture" we had, to a person, was a child-like grin. An uneasy stare, a sizable uneasiness, and with a toss of her head, she blessed us all. With a lilt of spirit that bounded like a dream over the sagebrush, she cleared the fence with one magnificent leap and dissolved into the evening.

Prayer life is becoming part of me. For Aquinas, "Virtue is a habit of the practical intellect." So, it would seem, prayer is *the* habit of consciousness. It is taking various forms. On the first rising, it is a "being with," a dialogical greeting of God, almost always in thankfulness. In the darkness of Vigils it is a matter simply of being enfolded, warmed, embraced, a "being in." At Lauds it is often an Abba repetition—a getting ready for the work day, in which the possibility of forgetting is greatest—preparation for "being by." The Eucharist is increasingly the unifying nourishment—an interpenetration of beings—a "being through." At meals, a simple grace of appreciation, a "being for." Through the day an ongoing conversation. Even siesta is becoming special. After lunch dishes, I take off my shirt and lie on a shed roof, warmed all over in a near spiritual way by "brother sun." Then Vespers—a quiet, coming home, an offering up to God the works of our hands, for better or worse. And then in bed; prayer is a goodnight, almost as if to a roommate, and the final trust of sleep, a "letting the world turn without you tonight." Three months ago all of this would have been anthropomorphic nonsense—indeed, downright embarrassing. Now it is okay, because prayer life seems to begin with a loss of self-consciousness over pseudo-sophistication. It isn't for the approval of anyone. It is okay. It is a beginning.

Friday, July 7

I spent all day doing yard work—cutting grass, trimming—frightening Fr. "E" that I would cut off some of his cherished aspen root saplings. Actually I did do one or two decapitations. It is a joy to beautify the place, especially to extend the yard further than it has been before. Creation and creativity are so much a part of my being that they are beginning to appear synonymous with spirit life. Berdyaev has been helpful in identifying the "image of God" in us as creativity, for it is the *Creator* God who said, "Let us make people into our image."

I have reflected further on the issue of memory. Redemption in part is the reliving of memories into new ones, ultimately into one memory that subsumes all others, purifying their meaning. This memory for the Jew has been "exodus," for the Christian the crucifixion-resurrection. As a child, the most painful, scared memories I have are those focused in the image of abandonment. To awake in a dark and creaky house to discover there is no one there but me. It was so graphic that it colored with grey possibility most other nights and some days. Therefore picture the redemptive meaning potential to spirit life experienced as "abandonment in God." It would be painfully hard, fraught with enormous resistance. But it would mean being freed to see that although no human relation is without potential for abandonment, that is all right, for there is one in whom abandonment means to be discovered, where to give up is to win, and where to lose the self is to find it. Incredible.

Brother "D" is increasingly invisible. I wish I knew more. There is something sad about the dwindling out, the unraveling, of that which was once so important. If only the monks could have a liturgy of closure that would enable celebration, regrets, new beginnings, and a quiet but hopeful closing of doors. But I fear that, instead, one day he will be gone.

Some of Brother "H's" folks are here. Each monk is permitted to invite his family to spend one week each year at the ranch house, complete with a party. One of the monks saw me yesterday and said, "If you don't get invited to the party this time I'm going to stuff my pockets, leave early, and you and I will have a ball together."

I just read an interesting passage in Merton: "Memory is corrupted and ruined by a crowd of 'memories.' If I am going to have a true memory, there are a thousand things that must be forgotten. He who remembers nothing but facts and past events, and is never brought back into the present, is a victim of amnesia."

I wrote messages to my two teaching colleagues who just don't know what to make of me. At the time it seemed to be a good thing to do; now I suspect they will only wonder all the more what I'm really up to.

Saturday, July 8

Right after looking out at the deep starred night, and the incredible glittering paint brush stroke of the Milky Way, I read in Merton about the need to keep one's eyes clean, one's ears quiet, and one's mind serene by working under God's sky. But what is one to do "if you have to live in a city and work among machines and ride in the subways and eat in a place where the radio makes you deaf with spurious news and where the food destroys your life and the sentiments of those around you poison your heart with boredom?" I say, "Amen." But his "solution" is hardly in the same class as his description. Nevertheless he is right: the called are those who can still hope for the healing silence, while all the others "do not even hope for it anymore" (*New Seeds of Contemplation,* p. 87).

In a conversation with Fr. "E," I mentioned my impression of monastic preaching—that it focused on the individual, on cultivating personal virtue, on seeing the problem solved "within," on changing attitudes, and on translating Divine helpfulness in terms of daily tasks. "Well," he said, "I'm preaching tomorrow, and your image will be confirmed." He encouraged me to say more. I spoke of the message monasticism seems to have for the modern world—especially for the affluent who show up every Sunday, good people "on the make" for profit, status, name, sophistication, culture—in a word, success. Monasticism has nothing to say if it cannot identify this acquisition as hollow and empty. It is then that the two defining characteristics of the new Trappism make sense: the healing meaning of solitariness of soul enwrapped in that silence which is the presence of God, and the new community of inclusiveness, eucharistically sharing in foretaste the goal of history—politically, economically, socially, culturally. The monastery to be itself is harbinger of the new, attempting to be born. He heard. The conversation was solid.

I remembered what a friend recently said of me: "You have a Protestant mind and a Catholic heart." I guess grace and Eucharist is a short-handed way of putting it.

At the Eucharist, we stood around the table with some visitors. As we said the responses, it was apparent how different the monastic tempo was from the others. Most visitors tend to run away with the words, instead of savoring each phrase. The pace of "getting done" versus that of "letting be." And the minute or two of silence at various places in the service tends to strain their endurance, severely.

Around 4:00, we went to the ranch house for spaghetti with Brother "H's" folks. The Abbot, prior, and new guest master made a point of inviting me. Of particular interest was the announced volley ball game. It was the first real game of any kind since my arrival. My past experience with men in volley ball involved heavy competition, spiced with setups flirting with extermination. How Trappist gentleness would cope with this promised to be interesting. Here are my "timeless" observations as a participant:

1. The picnic was totally open, with neighbors and friends invited.
2. Children were accepted into the game as equals, mistakes and all.
3. There was a dynamic operative so that as individuals drifted in and out, it was seen that the teams tended toward evenness.
4. There was a feigned competitiveness, a joking, a charging under the net after a play in pretended upsetness, a good-natured questioning of balls even obviously out-of-bounds—a general teasing, but always in advance of a play, never afterward.

73

5. No difference in status between Abbot, novice, brothers.
6. There was no criticism whatsoever, and only occasional advice to "weaker" players.
7. There were continuing invitations for spectators to join.
8. The game was genuine fun; we played until darkness made it absurd.
9. Afterward, there was no conversational replaying of the game.
10. Interestingly, as I write this a day later, I do not remember who won any of the games.

All in all, the game was impressively different.

Sunday, July 9

I couldn't resist. Around 3:30, during my second cup of coffee, I encountered ten cantaloupes in a line on the kitchen counter, with a sign indicating that they were not yet ripe. With a marking pen conveniently nearby, it was only natural that one of the melons would sprout a smiley face and a tin cup hat. I admit to an uncertainty as to how this would be taken. Two hours later, when I returned for breakfast, the rebellious cantaloupe had come alive—it now had a new hat, a cork pom-pom, and a dish towel dress. I may have started something: at None, Brother "A" sneezed in rapid succession midway through the reading of a somber psalm, but finished the last phrase without missing a beat—we split up in laughter. And somehow Brother "C" showed up for Vespers with one brown shoe and one black one. It is good that a community formed by the ritual of repetition is capable of sensing humor in the spontaneous infraction of that sameness. In fact perhaps it is only in a world of intention and expectation and promise that "pure" humor can occur—as delightful surprise. Elsewhere it often has the dynamic of harsh intrusion, even betrayal or undercutting.

I am sensing with Fr. "F" a delightful kind of friendship—

it is that rare specialness that makes one go for a walk one didn't intend to take, or naturally pick up two refills when one goes back for more, or seeks out the other to share a crazy culinary creation. It is an unconscious knowing what the other will like, a looking out for the other, without thinking about it. It's nice. I sometimes feel this with Br. "I" too.

I wanted to go for a hike, but we were hit with a heavy mountain thunderstorm, with cold, grey, ominous, howling winds. Here one begins to sense autumn in July. And somehow spirit life thrives on such rhythms—of dying and rising, cold and hot, inner and outer, newness and sameness, changing and constancy. Yet so much of today's culture is an artificial leveling out—air conditioning the hot, heating the cold, smoothing the rough, lighting the dark, shutting out the light. Such control has to be the foe of spirit. Without being swept by, done to, lured from, invaded with—one could make the fatal mistake of playing God. Nonetheless, I wanted to take a hike.

After early Vespers we gathered in the kitchen to make out individual versions of supper: everything from reheated leftovers to cream of wheat. Through mutual coaxing, the "dessert" became an endless bowl of fresh popcorn, spiced with salt and monastery stories.

Especially impressive was the verbal scenario of moving one of the Trappist cemeteries when the monastery changed locations. There was a kind of nonchalance about death; even its goriest details were no contest for halting popcorn consumption.

Monday, July 10

I am forever fighting with Merton. He rarely says things "right," yet is often so close that I would like to rewrite him. His treatment of the Christian as revolutionary is quite pale; but then later he strikes at the heart of the monastic awareness—the absolute emptiness, poverty, obscurity which holds the secret of joy because it is full of God. Yet he does not seem to be aware of how terribly revolutionary this is, for a person "suddenly loses his interest in the things that absorb that world, and discovers in his own soul an appetite for poverty and solitude." This is to turn American capitalism on its head, and to create people before whom the power of the American dream is dead. This is to be genuinely free, even if one does not know it.

Fr. "E" is leaving for a ten day meeting. I was touched when he asked me to assume his responsibilities for the lawn and especially his beloved trees. He gave me a detailed introduction to each of his tree friends and their special needs.

While I was mopping the refectory, two brothers gave me a quick course in the remembrance of things past. They showed me a stool about nine inches high, autographed on the bottom by the first monk to use it. It was a form of discipline by which one must eat his meal on the floor while sitting on the stool. This was "punishment" for such things as talking in the cloister, an error in judgment, the use of hand signs for theological discussions, etc. This conversation resulted in my first lesson in Trappist signs, a very realistic use of hands to convey about fifty basic needs or ideas. Before Vatican II, their use for more than the very essentials was disciplined.

The Abbot met with me for forty-five minutes before Vespers. He was pleased with my "spiritual progress," especially its spontaneous nature (rather than being forced), its variety, and its tendency to range throughout the day. He seemed ready now to work more closely with me in direction. He gave me six tapes on the Prayer of Centering, and went with me to the library to find two special books, to be read at the rate of several pages a day. One was a slender volume by an anonymous Carthusian called *They Speak by Silences;* the other, an Eastern classic, *Tao Te Ching.*

I think tomorrow morning I will use the library to reintroduce myself to some Eastern-type meditation, trying to get a better feel for Taoism, Yoga, Zen, and the two basic forms of Buddhism. The time with the Abbot was important, not only for the caring, but as a weekly review which helps me see that more has been happening to me than I recognize. I received a letter from a friend who said, "You have always been uniquely sensitive to the feeling tones and nuances and barely emerging insights in other people—with a kind of sixth sense—and have helped to give birth to those. I was less sure about your having that sense in relation to *you,* and somehow it sounds as if, someway, with the enabling power of what and who is around you, you are 'birthing' something new." I hardly know what to make of that, or to know if it is so. My prime uneasiness is if any change will have "staying power."

Tuesday, July 11

Today seemed to mark a third kind of breakthrough. During the last week I have been meditating on the cure of memory. Each of us is scarred by the past; but the active persistence of those scars rests in our remembrance now. Psychoanalysis is one method for re-remembering from the vantage point of distance. But spiritual re-remembering is, in addition, a process of reseeing. During Lauds I was swept again by the awareness that my scars of memory are the fear of being left, and the agony of being alone, and the craving to be free. This is no new insight, but now it was replete with faces and events. The insight came when I spontaneously prayed, "Do not leave me, to be alone all over again." There it was—projecting onto God the informing scars of memory. Do not do to me what "everyone" else ends up doing. The spiritual cure of memory, it would seem, turns the whole of that lifetime around—"Because you will never leave me, and even in my loneliness are behind the darkness, transform my memories, not by denying them but by permitting me to relive them within the certainty of your companionship." This insight came in a flash. I have difficulty trusting relationships. My way of dealing with them has been to "deserve them" by becoming socially and intellectually "capable." But that makes me the center, and it has the feel of Ecclesiastes—one relation comes into being, and another fades to another priority—there is nothing new under the sun. Therefore the new is when

77

recollection is transfigured in the light of Abba presence, and memory is rendered *only* memory. The question is how to let this awareness infect the unconscious regions of habit. Perhaps it is in being swept by the awareness that Jesus is the human face of the divine companionship.

I prayed for Brother "B" during the Prayers of the Faithful—one year since he made his first profession. Another brother prayed for Brother "D" who almost at that very moment was boarding a plane—he will not return. The last finality of a one-way ticket. Several of us talked spontaneously after Mass about our departed brother. It seemed that we had some "work" to do before closing that book. We then closed it. I believe it will remain closed.

Today was the feast of St. Benedict, the primary feast day of the Trappists. A special toasted cheese sandwich and beer supper was announced for 5:30. By 5:45 I had not been invited. Fr. "E" found me watering the trees and said they were waiting for me. In indicating that my former director had said that I was not to assume an invitation to anything, he simply said, "Brother 'D' has gone." It was a simple, warm supper. Especially impressive was a story that Fr. "F" had told; the monks asked him to repeat it for me. Quietly, humbly, he told in detail how, in his pilgrimage as a monk, he had been asked twice, rather emphatically, to leave the monastery because he did not have what it took. It occurred to me that these are the kind of failures that each of us has experienced; but it is rare indeed to have the courage to share them anywhere except in the isolated rehearsal room of our own wounded ego. He seemed unthreatened, without need either to defend himself or to provide alternative interpretations.

Wednesday, July 12

I think Merton is right: detachment is the basic requirement for spirit life. While he calls it the mystical death to all things created, he means letting go of possession as the criterion for meaning, of status as the criterion of being, and of power as the instrument of significance. It is an abandonment of the American values in order to be willing to be no one, to be insignificant, and to be unrecognized. Clearly God is the only way through which this could be possible. It is symbolic that almost every book I have read for the last week has something like this on the title page: "Translated from the French by a monk of Parkminister." Merton was never able to lose himself in this way. But those who are are incredible!

In Vigils we had a 3:15 A.M. "breakup." The brother was reading from "Rule of the Master," regarding the underclothing a monk should wear. It should be made, it seems, from "linsey-woolsey" (whatever that is). But the third repetition of this name in the sacred darkness was too much—we all cracked up. I think God must have enjoyed it too.

A fourth kind of breakthrough may have occurred today. Almost all reading that I have done indicates that one can expect darkness when prayer passes beyond the level of understanding and imagination. At that point prayer is no longer a relationship of thought or even experience, but of faith alone. Prayer in the end, then, is objective, not subjective. I have known that the anthropomorphic images characterizing my present prayer life are absurd, defying much that as a philosophical theologian I find even remotely acceptable. And *yet*, by faith alone, it would seem they are meaningful—not for understanding, not for picturing, not even for experiencing, but for their own sake, no matter what. This, in its own small way, must be prayer as the darkness of my own unknowing.

Thursday, July 13

During egg packing, Brother "H" and I brainstormed on options to full-time resident monasticism. We discussed the idea of an apostolate relation to the monastery by someone willing to be under discipline, whose work in the world furthered experimentation in and communication of the meaning of contemplation in a world of action. There should be an initial three month residency at the monastery under supervision, giving assurance that such understanding and practice of prayer has occurred that one will be able to "progress" in a self-directed way. Within six months he would apply for apostolate relation through a proposal that would describe his concrete apostolate. He would agree to a daily liturgical schedule, send quarterly reports to the Abbot, and spend one month each year in residency at the monastery. After three years, on unanimous vote of the monks, he would be eligible to become an apostolate member of the community. It was interesting to explore the idea, thinking, on the one hand, of my own situation, and, on the other, of Brother "H's" belief that the monastery has a responsibility to the world. He urged me to present it to the Abbot.

I learned first-hand today what one monk calls the "monastic factor" (bureaucracy). The Abbot made a new fence gate, but it sags. He designed a brace, made by another monk, given to me to install. It works, but the gate is twisted, and so only opens completely one way. Another monk has expressed negative feelings about the appearance of the gate. So I am to fix it, but only after the Abbot talks further with that monk. Today he gave permission to the monk to talk directly to me, and although he is not to help, I am to satisfy him. I worked out the options, he made the decision: a compromise between a twisted gate and a leaning post. Got it done, but it appears as if the assistant carpenter was a beaver. Hopefully a little weathering and we will have a satisfactory primitive monastic factor gate.

Have been earnestly involved in tree and grass watering now, but the biggest problem is not to interfere with Fr. "F's" sleeping, since he is bothered by sprinklers. Actually, all of this is excellent conditioning for nurturing a profound sense of humor.

Strange but the pickup truck got sick yesterday to the "tune-up" of $1,200. In the mail today came a check from a "friend" for $1,600. Guess the Holy Spirit added service charges.

Before Fr. "E" left for his trip, we discussed various approaches to spirituality. This whole field has seemed so overwhelming because, in part, its "ingredients" are not clear. What, for example, are the genuine options that seem available? These are the ones on which we agreed.

1. Recollection (concentration of one's powers in a unified activity).
2. Jesus prayer (as instrument for Presence)—prayer without ceasing.
3. Vocatives (names for calling upon God, especially helpful if the words are actually those used by Jesus, e.g., Elohim, Abba).
4. Abba repetition as tool for remembering.
5. Lectio Divina—sacred reading, especially of Scripture, as instrument of Divine address.
6. Mantra—repetitive words for stilling the mind to emptiness and rest, in preparation for God.
7. Prayer of centering (more later).
8. Petitionary prayer (prayer means "to ask").
9. Meditation—(literally it means the moving of one's lips), reflecting on the meaning of something read aloud.
10. Contemplation—being before something or someone (including God) with pure immediacy.
11. Eucharist—a mode of gathering life together as an offering to God, having it transformed and returned as grace (gift). It is the empowering rhythm informing with meaning the cosmos.
12. Dialogical prayer (conversation with God as companion).
13. Practicing the presence—substituting Christ as mediator in consciousness (between self and self) and in perception (between self and world).
14. Disciplining of will so as to be able to will nothing—i.e., so to turn off the mind as to become totally receptive.
15. Affective prayer—relation of feeling addressed to God and experienced as relationship.
16. The Jesuit-type exercises of imaginative re-creation of a Gospel scene.

17. Constant prayer, using breathing, or heartbeat, as unconscious continuation of a mantra.
18. Yoga—wholistic body centering with emphasis on breathing and posture.
19. Fasting.
20. Spiritual direction: a soul companion for life as pilgrimage.
21. Liturgical rhythms.

These are very different matters. Yet I found it helpful to write them as themes, around which there are clusters of variations.

I finished listening to the six tapes on the Prayer of Centering. It is a way of getting quickly into the heart of Trappist spirituality, which is contemplation. Since God is all around us and in us, the task of contemplation is to become open to this presence. All we can do is prepare, which means emptying the self in order to receive. While there are many obstacles, they center in two: (1) the mind as unending stream of thought; (2) the imagination as a perpetual motion picture. The presence of God entails not doing but being—to rest in God. Thus many "techniques" in the history of religions help discipline us to eliminate these activities by turning off the switch of the mind. This does not produce contemplation (union); we only prepare for what God may do according to his promise. The prayer of centering is another way of dealing with "mantra." One lets emerge a word, or very short phrase, especially a vocative for God. A favorite is the one used by Jesus—"Abba, Father." By repeating this, over and over again, the mind is given something to do, as a sort of "mindless preoccupation," and in slowing the speed of our repetition, thinking may stop all together. We are at perfect peace—empty yet full, doing nothing but savoring the immediacy of the present, without any concepts or images whereby one can even "know" that this is God. One does not have an experience—one *is* experience. Invasion by immediacy. This is the heart of contemplation.

Yet I find that turning off the mind is not enough, because

pictures continue to pass by. Without thinking, I am watching. My own technique is to form a triangle of my thumbs and first fingers. These are pressed to my forehead and cheeks until I experience a triangle of light. If it strays, by pressing it can be called back to the center. In time, my hands can be on my lap, and gentle pressure to each other is enough to recall the centered image. It is as simple and as difficult as that.

Several supplementary aids are these: begin the session with a short prayer asking precisely for what you want; find a comfortable place and position; if tense, think each part of one's body chronologically into peace, moving from the foot to the top of the head; take deep breaths, forcing them out, until deep and slowly rhythmic breathing takes over naturally. Discipline comes by setting aside a regular period of time, probably fifteen to twenty minutes, at least twice a day. And when time is up, come out of it slowly, perhaps in repeating thankfully the Lord's Prayer.

Actually this method is an expression of the fourfold monastic practice of lectio (scriptural preparation), meditatio (mental prayer), oratio (affective prayer), and contemplatio (union). *Cloud of the Unknowing* is the favorite book in this approach to spirituality.

Saturday, July 15

At 5 A.M. my contemplation was a breakthrough. It was contemplation, and I knew it. I checked my watch, believing I had been in the chapel for five minutes—I had been there over twenty. This helped me gain a perspective. I am not here at the monastery to read books, to do research, or to write scholarly articles, but to be shaped and disciplined in the spirit. Without planning it or being clear about it or being in control of it, it is happening. Amazing.

Today haying started in earnest—good crops, much winter snow, limitless irrigation. But when it was cut, hail began, and cold winds set in. Weird but exciting—to feel the rhythms of nature. Here one still is not in control. Life remains fragile, and thus sacred.

Now that the public is turned away at the entrance one mile from the monastery, I was assigned to take down the eight-foot-high fence surrounding the front of the monastery. In being cloistered, we now appear to be more open, with all the romance of a split log fence. Needing a crowbar, I searched in the boiler room. In the secular world such rooms are the citadel of macho existence, complete with girlie pictures and a revealing calendar or two. Suddenly I smiled, for lo and behold, scotch-taped to the wall near the boiler, was a picture of a sweet young thing. Some things, evidently, never change. But I looked closer, and my laughter became vocal. There, in the secularly traditional spot, was indeed a woman—the Virgin Mary.

The day had a different feel because my supervisor sat down with me to review what I had done during the week and think through what needed to be done, and he gave me the freedom to prioritize and get at it. One has much greater investment when one has a part in it. I was working now for the community. A real joy.

Sunday, July 16

I am midpoint in my Trappist residency. Last evening, during the rain, for no apparent reason, I went to the library and got out two books with pictures and commentary on Merton's life—one by his friend Edward Rice, one by John Howard Griffin. I also got a Merton introduction to life at Gethsemani. It was absorbing not only to enter again his personal life, but to see contrasting ways in which he was perceived. One interpreter emphasizes that he never left the monastic grounds for twenty-six years—except for one trip with the Abbot, another to a conference with Suzuki, and a number of visits to a nearby city for doctors' appointments. Another interpreter identified him as active in the world, seeing movies, speaking and traveling, with a constant stream of visitors. My fascination is leading me to read much that he wrote. He is beginning to emerge clearly as a solitary man of this world, claimed by craving, driven to search—Columbia to monastery to hermitage to Tibet. Evidently there was increasing tension with the Abbot, increasing disillusionment with American life in particular and the white race in general, heartache over the state of Christianity as an heroic life style, and frustration with the quality of monastic life, where economic production seemed more central than the contemplative search. Yet he was totally impractical, a dreamer, who needed to be cared for, had strong ego needs, and was romantic and fleetingly restless. He experienced upheavals of "impatience, resentment, disgust." He had his hermitage woods for joyful solace, but even here the shadow of death blew: "An unexpected chill comes out of the depths, and I breathe the cold air of darkness, the sense of void." He wrote while in California on his final trip that he would remain a monk *of* Gethsemani (not necessarily *at* Gethsemani?), and in a perfunctory letter from New Delhi stated that he was learning "for the community." But Rice is convinced he was not going to return, that his increasing interest in Buddhism meant his trip was a pilgrimage of "new steps" through Eastern immersion. This is why he had become concerned about money—for he was to be a hermit elsewhere, wherever that would be. Evidently in his eight days in Darjeeling in retreat preparation, and then under the supervision of a spiritual master of the original form of Buddhism in Tibet, he went into the steep hills of the forest and lived as a Buddhist recluse, deep in meditation. The pictures he took of the mountains are overpowering. And there, Rice would lead us to believe, was a real breakthrough for him in spiritual transcendence, a new step into what he knew not.

I went to sleep very much in the presence of Merton's life. For reasons not clear, my mood was one of great, almost overpowering sadness. After Vigils, in the near darkness, I completed his *New Seeds of Contemplation.* The ending in particular is some of his finest work; it seems to correlate with his own ending—his search for the cloud, as a "vanishing into God." The craving, the abyss, the being driven on for "rest in God." These are the meek who inherit the earth, for in renouncing it they alone can enjoy it. So then the world is seen as the realm of God's playing, and we, created in his image, become the artistic laborers who joyfully tend it. And in the incarnation he enters, excited to become friend. He becomes incarnate in the inner self of all. Therefore our decision is whether we wish to become aware. Through us, God is exile and pilgrim in his own creation, involved as dancer in his garden. This cosmic dance we catch in echoes—alone in a starlit night, or beneath the migrating birds in autumn, or with children as children, or witnessing the solitary splash of an old frog. All is emptiness, and the informing silence is the wedding feast, the joy of which nothing can stain. Whether or not we want it, it beats in our very blood—and we are invited.

Joy, yes, but sadness—deep, metaphysical sadness. Never enough, never quite. In a way Merton was a little kid whose favorite word was "Boy!" He was a naive sophisticate, alienated not by the world but by *this* world. My fascination with Merton I now understand. In him I see much of myself. And so now I am alone in a monastery, yet only an echo away from the Aspen world of buying and selling the creation. Strangely the incredible beauty of this world, and the demonic condition of our doing, gives rise to the craving for another world, of Being. Forever and ever—*damn!* It is too much. The sun just hit the tip of the mountain.

In a way this day has been another breakthrough. Prayer really is *the* life style of the Christian. The mind of Christ is the mind at prayer—it is the way of standing in God before God with God. It is all-inclusive. While previously for me prayer was one possible activity among many, now nothing else matters; not to be involved in it is not to be a Christian. Yet prayer is pluralistic. It is not just one mode, so that one dare not make contemplation the only or "highest" form of prayer. Merton's final search was for absorption. But in this life we must turn from the mountain, and return. And not grudgingly. And yet . . .

Monday, July 17

Today by letter a friend asked, "Are you retreating more and more into the spiritual, apart from the more ordinary where most of us are?" It was strange to hear my own answer. It had to do with scars. I was not retreating from life, nor from the inner city to which I am deeply committed, nor from the plight of this country, which gives me agony without respite. But I want a grounding in the solitary center of my being, beyond the hurt that undoes, in a grounding sufficiently certain that I do not get in the way of what I must be and do. It is a matter of not being easily undone—strength, serenity, confidence without the need of excessive and romantic hope. I think Merton would understand—Merton the mature little boy.

The weather has been strange, yet important. Soul seems to come not out of controlled situations but out of living in the midst of uncontrolled rhythms with which one must cope. Sunday we were hit by a hailstorm that made work sporadic and dependent. Today a storm blew from the mountains until the windows rattled, and one could mount serious concern for the belltower. Then suddenly, as quickly as it had come, came the quiet and rolling grey—an evening of the unknown but expectant.

I received a difficult letter from home. Three of my children—all of whom are either first or second in their high school classes—are learning almost nothing positive, losing much sense of the correctness of language, and are settling down to the inner city apathy and hard endurance of the poor white ghetto where we live. The question was put straight: What is the responsible act? Proposed was a suburban private school—I cringed! The very "classism" of such an escape! It would cost over $3,000 a year, which is more than the total income of many in our neighborhood. In the face of this, although I know better, I was flooded with the thought of spirit life as luxury. I read in *Time* magazine about a recent TV documentary on the slums of Newark and New York—evidently it was devastating. And a letter from my colleague stated, "As for the international scene, it is deteriorating rapidly not only at the point of détente, but in South Africa, the Mideast, balance of payments, decline of the dollar and a stepped-up arms race ... In other words, we cannot take much comfort from political life or movements these days." Yet, of course, without spirit life, where is the centering that keeps from undue compromise, the fundamental base for outlasting a demonic time that might require radical surgery for a condition possibly terminal? It is a terrible thing to be bitten by the living God.

Meanwhile, back at the monastery, a brother sensed my struggling, and asked me to go fishing. I asked my resident "master." The answer was a clear "no," for reasons unclear.

Tuesday, July 18

It is 4:00 A.M. The moon is totally full, and its impact is aesthetic, spiritual, and therapeutic. One senses it in the monks. I just returned from getting a cup of coffee, and the monastery no longer has the usual feel of being deserted. Brothers are strolling in the cloisters, almost like spring, when life and beauty are too much for one to be still. So it was in its own way last evening. Just before bedtime, I shifted the sprinklers for the night; as I stood listening to the water, I looked up. A deer was walking out of the alfalfa, onto the lawn, and walked to within ten feet of me, as if asking to drink. We talked for maybe half a minute, then I slowly backed away, and he had his drink before retiring. Gentle.

That gentleness was on the bulletin board. The note began, "Goldie died today." Goldie is the little dog owned by an old widow in the ranch down the road. Goldie died, and now the woman is all alone. The monks will pray for both of them. And they promised to help her find another dog companion.

I found it very difficult writing to a friend who innocently asked, "What is happening to you?" In fact I had started the letter several times, and finally put it off. There has been so much.

This morning I tried again. I mentioned the Province Beyond the River, the insatiable metaphysical craving that (known or unknown) is the quest for God within God's quest for us. I mentioned Merton's conclusion in *Seven Storey Mountain*, where he speaks of the Christ of the burnt "men." I spoke of us as the scarred and wounded folk. I remembered the anonymous Carthusian who spoke of being wounded by God with a wound that will never heal, so that through it God may enter the heart of our being. And then I spoke of the pilgrim, and the exiled God, dancing and beckoning in his own creation. And, of course, the old frog and the new deer. Words ... words ... Today I read from St. Bernard. Among much, he said, "I learn as much or more from running brooks than from written books."

Wednesday, July 19

Today I changed my sheets. No big thing, except that the fresh ones were dark brown, homemade from a heavy-duty sack type material. There was something very right about them. They made sleep feel integral to the earth.

During meditation, I realized that Merton's "old frog" isn't enough, because he just ate a fly. The Zen awareness of the now in all its immediacy is only a beginning, a mere glance at the power of being. The "more" is forced by the perennial magpie right outside my window; in all her black and white splendor, she is perched in a watch of death. It will be all over for anything moving within the range of her quick eye. She just pounced. What can one say?

In taking down an old fence and told to store the wood in an open field, it seemed that a better place would be as a rough bench under some aspens overlooking the mountain. It took fifteen minutes to build, but far more time to get permission. When Br. "C" and I tried it out after lunch, he said, "This is the first time in my fifteen years here that we have ever been able to sit under a tree." I came to my cell, picked up a book, and read, "One's neighbor is an icon of God. So is one's own self."

Father "F," our resident fisherman, was in a "liturgical bind" this morning as he celebrated. The eucharistic prayer read, "And we thank you for the fish in their freedom within your streams." Eyes turned toward him; he never blinked. But for the first time in a week, he did not go fishing today.

Around a family style dinner of toasted cheese sandwiches and salad, Br. "A" shared with us his enthusiasm about a recent conference on music. We listened to some records and sang a bit from new books that he bought. A gentle time. This is my family, for the time being.

Thursday, July 20

I spent the earliest hours writing letters to my family: the sorrow of separation, of growing up, of doubts, of wondering, of justifying this period in separation from them. I wanted so much to touch and to let them know how very dear they are to me. Hours later there was still a heavy sense of sadness.

Ironically around 6:15 P.M. one of the monks told me that three people were outside and would be coming to Eucharist to see me. What a surprise—three members of my family. Afterward we bubbled on and on. Br. "A" arranged it so that I can have Sunday morning off to be with them. While we were outside, four of the monks, independently, came out to greet them. It is clear how beautiful is the experience of being loved. And at sunset, as I was moving the hoses, my deer friend came to see me again.

Friday, July 21

Thoughts about the rich intersections of my life bring me to the tentative conclusion that the deepest times now are the moments immediately surrounding waking (spontaneous gratitude), the Eucharist (overwhelmed by presence and the irreversibility of what is happening to me here), and my cell (especially the moonlit silence of the early morning).

Comments last night indicated how few of "us" there seem to be. My family found the Eucharist "a little interesting" but "not their thing." Yet it is the feeding center of my life. This may call for Bonhoeffer's "secret discipline," or what the writer of Matthew meant by "closet prayer." To be fed while living a life style not pietistically (observably) different from those around you—what is different is *where* you are, *why*, the *goal*, and the inner integrity in presence which is the emptied self.

I finished Merton's last work, *Asian Journal*. I am about ready to make my peace with him. I believe I understand. The difficulty rests not in his writings, but in his life. When he left for Asia, he clearly was returning to a home where he had never been before. He was literally in search of a new hermitage, one of near total isolation and quiet (but periodically he "would come out"), of which Alaska or the western redwoods were his favorite options. He craved to "disappear into God," yet he thrived on the very popularity that he loved to lament and flee. He was a little boy, excited by new adventure, impossibly romantic and naive, yet never so much himself as before an open fire, alone with a cup of tea, able to express it all with the one word "contentment." His love-hate relation with even the mountain Kanchanjunga (28,000 feet) is indicative—blaming her for being a postcard, angered by her playing hide and go seek with him, and yet he could not help photographing her continuously in the hopeless hope of "coming to terms with her." When he looked back from the taxi window for the final time, she insisted on staying hidden, the symbol really of "a great consent to be and not be"—there it is. And so I look out in the moonlight at "Silver Mountain," "my" mountain, on which I almost lost my life several years ago in an avalanche. The craving to climb her "impossible" west side, where another time a forfeiture of spirit did me in, yet knowing each time I see her that such a contest is moving daily in her favor, as time runs out on my strength. I know Merton, well.

Today had something of that same absurdity. For the first time in one and a half months I was permitted to leave the monastery land. With two others, we made a "pilgrimage" to Wingo Junction! It was one mile from the road leading up to the monastery, with a population totally missed by the last census. Its claim to fame is a railroad siding, with one box car for us, one for the lumberyard, and one mysterious one, unopened and unknown. My guess is it was the stake-out for the local game warden. Two trips, a late lunch, three tired backs later, and we had taken ubiquitous egg cartons to their temporary monastic home. On our final trip we composed a song—"The Wingo Junction Blues."

That evening I read that prayer rests in becoming again like little children, the "anawim"—simple, loving, trustful, joyous. In the morning the Abbot said that a phone call had come for me, but that he had discouraged the caller. His way of putting it was, "I'll help you filter out the world."

Saturday, July 22

I found myself in the interesting position of representing the monastery. In working on the entrance road, I became the curiosity target of tourists. One classic dialogue: "How come the monastery is closed to visitors? It wasn't this way before." "So that we can concentrate more on our reason for being—solitude, silence, contemplation." "Then how come you're able to talk to me." "Because our dictum is: Speak only when it improves the silence. I had hoped you would. Have a good day." I found myself using humor, assuming that others recognized its truthful absurdity. How else does one deal with such questions as "Why are you here?" or "What do you do?"—"I am in charge of rain," or "I watch things grow," or "I make sure the mountains don't move." I believe I only confirmed the perspective of most tourists coming to buy jam or to see a real monk; we are all crazy. They may be right.

The Abbot has been trying to get together with me for a week. We finally made it around twilight. In its own way, it marked my next breakthrough. We talked about the prayer of centering and decided to try it together. It begins with relaxing, asking for what you want, twenty minutes of "resting" in the ground of being by using a mantra to keep bringing oneself back to the center, shutting down mental activity, and refusing to be pulled into the images of the imagination as they go by. Previously my results were strained and dispersed. This time was strangely different. At times I would think of things, but now I was *watching* the mind do it. Mountains and green meadows floated toward me, but I let them go by without walking in them or climbing them. My relaxing was so complete that my arm slipped from my lap and my head kept falling forward as if asleep. Yet I was alert, watching it all happen. The word for it is "deep." One senses it most in "coming out." It is like a waking up, a stretching, a blinking of the eyes, a reorientation, a beginning again. But even more, I experienced it as a total reorientation. As I left and "floated" down the cloister, I was in a fog but everything was right there, not vague. Or better put, everything was invaded by a mist of feeling—a feeling of gentleness. I walked quietly, carefully, as if on tiptoe. It would have been difficult to focus had I needed to talk. In the kitchen I watched the water boiling with a kind of quiet delight. People came and people went, but I stayed there, forever. I tasted orange juice, played with a beautifully green salad with orange-red dressing, chewed granola for at least a year, and took it with me on a walk in the grass. I poured a little milk as a sharing with a wild flower. This was a trip—really it was. There was no desire for anything else but to be "in God." As I think about it, these are the right words. It is not so much being "with God" (as in the Abba repetition or in practicing the presence). It is being "in" God, or "as" the creation in the creation . This "mood" of gentle guest persisted through Vespers and into sleep.

Sunday, July 23

Sunday dawned as a beautiful, cloudless day. There was a deep happiness in hiking into the surrounding mountains with some of my family. But I must confess doing the ultimate Trappist sin—we cooked and I ate two hot dogs. We hiked the high ridges, only to find roads cut by a bulldozer from the other side, preparatory to selling building lots where one can "watch" monastic peace.

The public Eucharist was difficult. Fr. "F" had told me he was going to preach on evil. We shared a bit about it, but evidently there was no communication. I disagreed with almost all of the homily, and at points was near anger. It clarified the theological foundation for my uneasiness about many monastic homilies. Evil of the physical sort, he said, is no particular problem. It is simply nature working itself out. With that quick answer, the agony of countless theologians was swept away—hurricanes, cancer, death—"just nature's way." Moral evil is the problem, he said, and it is like an iceberg; since we see only one-tenth of it, there is no way to solve it in this life. But as Christians we know there is no dualism, no evil powers other than just the privation of the good. We know that everything will work out, and as a matter of fact Jesus himself did not seem overly perturbed about the whole matter. (How can he say this, when in crucifixion Jesus screamed of death as abandonment by God?) It followed in his closing prayer that we must "be content with our lot." A great prayer for Aspenites who indeed should be delighted with their lot, even literally. But for the poverty class, such words are the opiate indeed of the people. It is not hard to see how hundreds of monastic sermons can follow in which religion becomes the development of inner virtues.

I felt so very alone afterward, disappointed, but, more, abandoned. It did not help my openness in reading of Merton's explorations into Zen. I understand what he means in claiming that Zen is not a theology but an openness to the Ground of Being, a way of seeing, not explaining, of being shaken from the false-ego that divides all things into subject and object. The self is lost when it operates within the false consciousness that sees life as the grasping and manipulation of things, competing with others for the limited possessions which give power and status. Precisely. And thus its revolutionary nature—the United States is founded precisely on this false consciousness, breeds it, rewards it, defines authenticity by it, and rises up in the "titanic efforts to build the world according to their own desires ..." And yet, Merton's efforts do precisely what he says we should not do. He "demythologizes" Christian theology *into* this awareness. As I stood alone in the chapel this morning, while the people were outside congratulating the preacher, the thought swept me: there can be no reconciliation with this Ground, this Abyss, this Source, without Jesus Christ as the crucified God in the midst of history. The cross is not just a demythologized symbol for self-negation preparatory to this new Oneness. God must be the One struggling against the powers and principalities, with us. While the battlefield in part is the "soul," it is so because the conflict is cosmic, on the plane of history. In no way, then, dare we identify the kingdom of God as "within." It is within in order that it may be without. The spiritual struggle is not for its own sake, any more than for "heavenly reward." Religion can accommodate itself to "life" only by forfeiting history. Nor is it reducible to changing people so that society will be changed. It is when one grasps the profound interpenetration of society and self that evil in all its supra-personal force is encountered. Then our cry becomes known—it is not simply for the Ground of Being, but for that Ground *who takes sides in history.* It is he who does not cause the cross, or watch the cross, but is the cross. "Suffering against" by "suffering with"—the cross is not only in the middle of history but in the center of God. Without Christ as the crucified Emmanuel, there is no reconciliation with the Creator Ground.

It is really hard to believe, but at twilight I went to my window to draw the drapes. There was my deer friend, watching me through the glass.

Monday, July 24

In reading in the Taoist "scripture" I came upon a central thought which seemed to catch the dilemma that plagued me yesterday. It is a statement that can be so right, and yet so dangerously wrong: "The world is ruled by letting things take their course. It cannot be ruled by interfering." The deep distress that I am feeling is that here, where so much deep remaking is occurring in me, is where there is only an eye blink distance from the base for everything against which my life must be a "no."

Suzuki claims that Merton's description of Zen "emptiness" still has to do with God the Creator and is not the Zen emptiness of the Godhead. Creation is not in time, but out of inexhaustible nothingness, eternally. For Suzuki, Christianity is affective, personal, and dualistic (preserving the difference between self and God); Zen is non-affective, non-personal, non-dualistic. I think Merton tried too hard to resolve this difference, and, ultimately, as he admitted, "simply avoided a thorny theological problem." The metaphysical question cannot be dodged, and in doing so Merton increasingly assumed the Zen metaphysical foundation. It is amazing how much like Paul Tillich Merton became.

To translate such thinking into practice seems to mean affirming three types of prayer, resisting the tendency to synthesize them or reduce one to the other. The first is the intuitive awareness of the groundless foundation of being, an imageless emptying, resting in God, letting be in the sustaining power of Being Itself. There is also a second, the prayer of Emmanuel— the eternally enfleshed companion, the incarnate presence within us as the gift of baptism, the One who displaces the me in the I-me relation which is consciousness. It is the God-with-us against the powers of evil and death. If the first type is illustrated by the prayer of centering the second is grasped by Br. Lawrence's practice of the presence. The third, that of the Spirit, is being grasped by the intentional dynamic sweep of creation as the *élan vital*, not in cosmic and eternal repetitions but the promised call luring all forward into transfiguration. Only together do we have the good news—that orientation toward the creativity of the Groundless One as Emmanuel, calling us as co-creators in the forging of soul and the completion of creation under promise. Thus the "will" of God needs to be rethought along lines of beauty and the artist, rather than those of obedience and the lawgiver.

The Abbot reported that in the use of centering prayer one sometimes gains psychic release, for in that kind of profound resting the repression of past traumas is eased, analogously, to sleep, but with the creative clarity of consciousness at peace.

At Eucharist I prayed for a friend who is finding his Ph.D. thesis debilitating. Afterward, Br. "A" made the helpful suggestion that prayers of intercession, while often triggered by something concrete, are helpfully universalized and related to the Gospel for the day. I suspect that to take to heart that suggestion would be to pray for those who are searching for wisdom but seem caught in the methodologies of knowledge, particularly my friend; may they so sense your Spirit that they may know that yoke which is easy and that burden of meaning which is light.

Tuesday, July 25

This afternoon two of us were sent onto the high mesa. The sporadic rain has sufficiently dampened the hay bales so that many are beginning to mold. Thus for three glorious hours we turned over about a thousand bales; the beauty was to walk the fields, feeling the sounds of boots in grass, being able to see an expanse of 360°, yet be surrounded by mountains. Snow, the gurgling of water, birds, the quiet sounds of cattle, warm sun on bare skin, the clouds playing games as blue and grey and yellow passed in unexpected sequence. To be caught up in rhythms not of one's own making, to participate, to be wholly alive, without remainder. Then to get into the pickup, and bounce home content, with a warm tiredness in every limb.

What a contrast to this morning. While I was oiling the machinery, a neighbor woman came for eggs. After getting them, we walked to the car. She opened it and continued to talk for a long time. And from the car came noise—incessant, persistent, penetrating—the endless beat of repetitive music, and the sterile voice of ritualistic selling. I felt being done unto, trapped. It isn't simply noise versus silence. It is the contrast of sounds and rhythms, and thus of dance. The peace I felt when her talking car left was not really silence—it was what the bluebird said outside the window. Silence is what is necessary in order to hear.

As I was entering my cell at evening, Br. "C" motioned to me. He had been waiting. He had spent part of the day cleaning so that he could share his cell with me. The experience was rare, caring, gentle. We silently looked at his life—pictures, desk, chair, blanket, postal cards, window view. He smiled and said quietly as I left, "I knew you would like it."

Hemingway knew well the pearls of such moments—the fish well caught, the bull well fought, the bottle well drunk. But life floundered for him, "a dirty trick," for there was no string, no promise, on which to connect the pearls. Somehow, as I lay in the stillness, it all seemed to fit.

Wednesday, July 26

Since the split rail fence in front of the monastery is complete, the old railing from parking lot to the entrance was judged unnecessary and inappropriate. I was given the task of elimination. That entailed a sledgehammer and a hacksaw, with a burning torch lurking in the mind as possibility. I felt a sadness. Someone had built the railing by anchoring steel bars in concrete, bolted with large hardware. It was built to last. And now, years later, comes the wrecking crew, and what was such thorough work against time suddenly becomes a nuisance. And so, too, will come a time when someone will lament with real wonderment why anyone had taken out irreparably what I took out. Nothing is so essentially anchored to our center as our work—and nothing from our hands seemingly lasts. This, just as deeply as the craving in our depths, is an eschatological cry. If all things shall be as if not, then life and history are equally nightmares. Does resurrection apply to the work of our hands, to the dreams of our imagination, and to the unshared feelings of our shrouded souls?

Thursday, July 27

I am impressed by the degree to which wildlife seems to sense the gentleness of the monastery and that they have nothing to fear. Deer visit freely, with their innate curiosity freed to express itself. Last evening a large rabbit came on the lawn about ten feet from my window, stretched out full length on the grass, and promptly went to sleep.

I have wanted to immerse myself in this monastic experience, not to stand outside it in judgment. But today, before I feel that the appropriation is solid, I received a letter forcing some troublesome questions. It was a letter from one who has tasted the craving, and has experienced being "on the other side," "moving toward a presence that somehow corresponds to that all-encompassing, elusive, ever-present ontological craving for more, for completion and fullness, for Be-ing." But now her political and feminist developments have brought increasing alienation from the language and assumptions of Christianity in general and Catholicism in particular. She is not turning either from the craving or from the spiritual experience. What, at least in part, is at stake is the total masculinity symbolized by my experience here. I can no longer avoid the fact that this is a community of men, eucharistically served exclusively by men, celebrating a very virile God and his Son, united by a Spirit called "he." Women who come are carefully but kindly segregated, and the all-important Virgin Mary remains Virgin, pedestaled and elevated beyond the likeness of women. Indeed, I have not yet observed here any awareness of the totally masculine language of the liturgy—"for us men and our salvation." She states it well: "The language no longer speaks to me simply because I am not included in it. So what am I to do?"

And so she, an ex-nun, is struggling, as indeed she must, for new language and symbols that incorporate this monastic experience, but with integrity. Actually the language is only symptomatic, for sexism invades the very concepts themselves, both of Scripture and tradition (the Church "Fathers"). She has found some help in Mary Daly's shift from thinking of God as noun to verb, thereby rejecting naming as owning. For her, if God incarnate means "he" (i.e. Jesus), this revelation cannot be either exclusive or normative. Thus one must move away from "final" revelation to a process of moving "toward" relationship with and understanding of God.

All of this gives me an urgency to discover and read that part of history not only excluded by Christianity but labeled pagan. The deities of Canaan against which Israel raged and from whom they "liberated" land, crops, cattle, and women were feminine, the religion of sensual worship, of reverence for the earth, of relational divinity, of the joyous affirmation of sexuality. I began reading Stone's *When God Was a Woman*. It is a fascinating study of the basically sexist distinction between Jewish culture-religion and that of the Canaanites. She claims the conquest to be far more political than religious, and the later Jewish and Christian religions more syncretistic than realized. This seems confirmed by my recent reading of Scripture, for it is hard to conceive a more virile, machismo operation than the invasion of Canaan, complete with Yahweh's part played by Bear Bryant: "Our concern is not how to play—there is only one way to play: TO WIN." And then, the nerve of the "fathers," having rejected and vilified the whole, to come back and assume much under new names. Even the word "Easter," the central Christian holiday, comes from the goddess Oesyer, whose symbols were the egg and rabbit; Christmas too had its origin in matriarchy. Such heavy thinking was re-echoed by my family on Sunday, when one of them said after Mass: "The female half of the race is a significant portion not to be heard."

100

The introduction to Psalm 135 appearing in the psalter for Eucharist this morning only made things worse. It suggested that we "spiritualize" the idea of the "promised land" to which the psalm refers. But isn't demythologizing here as immoral as rendering the holocaust of the Jews in Germany a "spiritual" message that God asks total self-giving of each believer? And positively, if one rejects the promised land as goal in history, has Christianity not abandoned creation and history for the inner regions of the disengaged self? So disengaged, the rationalization that follows is well identified by my friend: "Christianity seems to pose no contradiction for the men who are responsible for raping and ruining the mountains, lakes, rivers, and animals for a profit—they can do it and still be 'good Christians.' " Her search is the effort to unite the best of "Catholicism, feminism, and American Indian spirituality," for "implicit in all three are reverence for life, ecology, cooperation, simple living, etc. These values are incompatible with corporate capitalism and technology for its own sake."

The issue at stake here can no longer be put aside. We must cringe and pray for forgiveness requiring centuries of penance. I was near paralyzed by the epistle reading for last Tuesday, imagining the terrifying damage it has done over the centuries: "Wives should regard their husbands as they regard the Lord, since as Christ is head of the Church and saves the whole body, so is a husband the head of his wife, and as the Church submits to Christ, so should wives to their husbands, in everything" (Eph. 5). May God forgive our "god."

Friday, July 28

The daily dynamics of living seem strangely capable of bringing out regrettable characteristics in oneself. Yesterday the cousin of one of the monks came to be a resident for one year. Today I am aware, with some pain and even more resentment, that he was immediately assigned to a cell (next to mine), began by being given a seat in choir, was taken to town for a ride during the weekly shopping trip, and while I was uninvited he attended the community meeting tonight. For all my supposed progress in spirit life, I do not know how to handle this, even though, as I write it, it seems so petty, so insignificant, indeed childish. I must keep clear in myself the perspective of what I am truly about. We, the people, are such a frail bunch. It seems to center in acceptance, and that is what redemption is about. Acceptance beyond the point of recall is what alone can quiet our innate need to justify ourselves, proving that we count more than anyone else, anywhere—or at least as much.

Saturday, July 29

In walking the road to the eggery, I saw a deer in the meadow who decided that I was passing between her and home. So with great caution, but even greater grace, she "outdistanced" me to the fence, and watched from the polite distance of the hill. I never tire of deer; when she leaped the fence, something deep within me leaped too. For the rest of the morning, in the midst of machinery and near mechanical chickens, I reflected upon the need for the shapes and rhythms of nature to structure and ignite and move the human spirit. There is something wrong when electric lights forbid the experience of night for chickens, and tin walls deny them the seasons. But even more wrong is the human life of plastic pretense within controlled environment. Ironically, when I returned for lunch, Br. "C" was having a one person revolution against a turquoise plastic waste can in the sacristy. "It is sacrilegious!" So without either discussion or permission, he demoted it to the kitchen, where with liturgical feeling he threw garbage into it.

There was a letter waiting from one of the two colleagues to whom I had written, expecting no response. It was warm, appreciative, honest. I wrote back inviting the attempt at gauging our relation by the future rather than the past. It is difficult, on both sides, to re-establish trust when it has been shaken. It is even more difficult to understand in relationships how two persons can both read the basis for mistrust from the same data. Yet this is so, over and over again; there seems to be no place to stand from which to see objectively. Risk seems to be the price for admission to intimacy, but risk as response—this is the religious factor called "grace" that makes all the difference.

In the evening, a passage from Rahner seemed to summarize my growth thus far. "He who has honestly resolved to seek the love of God may be said to possess that love already in his heart. For that very resolution is a proof that the grace of God has descended into the depths of his heart to kindle there a longing for God's love" (*On Prayer*). Here is the paradox characterizing prayer and the Christian life—more is less, to have nothing is to be full, to long is to be longed for, to be haunted implies a "by whom," and to yearn for a love still unknown is to have been found.

Sunday, July 30

Morning dawned with the earth very moist and very fresh. I was told later that we had a huge thunderstorm and lightning. I heard absolutely nothing. I must have been very tired or very much at peace.

"Church" seemed unusually noisy, and afterward the waves of buzzing from the visitors talking to the monks in the novitiate lasted unusually long. Two well-dressed Aspenites were engaging the Abbot. The only words I heard were, "Zen really scares me." "Oh, not me. I love it. I really do. It makes me feel so good!" It seemed as if I were hearing a late movie recut of T. S. Eliot's *The Love Song of J. Alfred Prufrock:* "In the room the women come and go/talking of Michelangelo."

I spent the morning in the sun, reading about the Jesus prayer. The prayer itself has many versions (e.g., the one word "Jesus"), but the form most useful in terms of rhythm is, "Lord Jesus Christ, have mercy on me." On the assumption that we are a physical-spiritual unity, to pray from the heart is to do so physically. This becomes literally possible by correlating the two phrases of the prayer with the beat of the heart, or the process of breathing. By practicing this physical/mental correlation, one establishes a rhythm that continues even in the subconscious when one is involved with other things, even sleep. It can thrust itself into consciousness, or can be called forth intentionally—but in each form it witnesses to "Christ within us." This companionship is named at baptism, and through the Jesus prayer is shaped as conscious awareness. The secret of the Gospel hidden for ages, according to St. Paul, is precisely this—"Christ in us." This process has the possibility of making other aspects of life into "symbol acts"—identifying a necessary act with a metaphorically suggested meaning. For example, the hymn "Breathe on Me, Breath of God" makes explicit the metaphor latent in breathing as the gift of life itself. By establishing this meaning-correlation by practice, necessary acts become themselves "automatic" expressions of sacramental meaning, making "prayer without ceasing" a possibility.

There seems to be a correlation between the Jesus prayer and what I have been attempting with the "Abba repetition"—to substitute, for the "me" in the I-me dialogue of consciousness, the presence of God. This reconstitution of consciousness is a near-literal understanding of "Christ in us."

This helps distinguish the two major types of prayer. The prayer of centering (using a mantra) is the non-verbal, non-imaged prayer of resting in the Ground of Being, in unity and oneness, rejecting all distinction, all activity, all consciousness, all dialogue. It is a restorative venture. The use of the Jesus prayer, however, is related to the Creator God who has become incarnate—Emmanuel, companion, God with us. The focus here is not unity but relational presence. It has both its active and resting forms, analogous to friends who interact as well as enjoy wordless presence with each other. Either way, the distinction of self and other persists.

We had supper at sunset, using for the first time the aspen grove in front of the monastery. It was good-natured, teasing, sacramental, sharing, family. It led quite naturally to thought of other spots adjacent to the monastery buildings that could be "sacramentalized" by our noise presence—and, with it, the mountains themselves.

Monday, July 31

Learning the varieties and practices of prayer is exciting, but can they sustain creatively one's total focus for the next thirty years or so? I truly don't know.

Around 6 P. M. I was in the kitchen, eating my supper in courses as other ingredients were cooking. One of the brothers came in to find someone to stand near the eight-foot-deep pit they had dug to repair a broken water main. The Prior was in the pit, and they wanted someone around in case it should cave in. I said I would, but a second brother told me to finish my supper; he would do it. Then a second question: "Do either of you know what a torque wrench is?" I did. So I went to the barn for the wrench and socket equipment. When I returned the Abbot and others were watching the operation, with justified apprehension. As Vespers approached, I continued to work with the two brothers while the others went to chapel. "Pray for us." "You can trust that we will." It was a sloppy, muddy business. After finishing, we climbed the hill to the tank to turn on the water. When I came down, a brother was waiting. He drew me aside and said that from now on I should not eat in the kitchen but in the refectory so that others would not be tempted to talk to me. Several others, he said, had echoed the same concern. And I should not have missed Vespers, at least not without his permission, for my stay at the monastery could become a farce by being led away from my central purpose. I asked if there were any other things I had done which made him think so. "No, I'll tell you if there are; but it is the first time that can begin patterns." Just then, a brother asked if I could drive him to the far field to get the jeep. This seemed to confirm for him the logic of the criticism I had received. I asked permission, and was told pleasantly: "Certainly." He added, "See what I mean?" I thanked him for his concern, drove the brother into the gathering silence, and remained awake most of the night.

How does one "properly" react to this? *My* logic said "injustice." I figured it out—I have attended approximately 240 services since coming here, without missing one until tonight, missed so that I could be helpful to the community by crawling around in a mud hole in threat of collapse. "But from now on ..." My feelings bordered on the petty, interlaced with the "I wish I would have said" syndrome. I felt so human; and for the first time I saw the wisdom of monastic training—in turning one's spiritual welfare over to a "guide." Yet I smarted from the subjective dangers. How important, and yet so impossible for me—for reasons as undeniably good as bad. As I practiced self-justification, I intellectualized that there seems to be here an internal conflict between the solitary silence of the way things used to be, and the community of friendly exchange; between the hierarchical authority of command and obedience, and the new corporate and informal basis for decision making. I felt caught when I least expected it, for reasons I least thought applicable. The "monastic factor" and the "human factor" were playing badminton in my psyche.

Tuesday, August 1

We awoke at the regular time, checked the sky for clarity, did Vigils, and drifted toward the kitchen for solitary preparations for an all-day hike to Williams Lake. I had negative feelings about being in the kitchen, especially when other brothers were talking. How does one neutralize such feelings? By the scheduled departure time (5 A.M.), the stars were covered, and there was occasional lightning in the west. This split the "delegation," and a decision was made to wait until 6 A.M. By the time I reached the parking lot at 6, the decision had already been made. Three of the group did not want to risk the weather, and it was assumed that I would go with the four who did. So as the

106

five of us started out by pickup truck, we were greeted alternately by rain, a spectacular sunrise, and hail. This was a harbinger for the day. The road into the mountains deteriorated from poor to impossible to unbelievable, until "miraculously" we arrived at the beaver ponds, majestically overlooking Haystack Mountain, Mount Daly, and Capital Peak. We hiked three miles through mist forests to Williams Lake. The next hours focused on the sky, as it put on an amazing show of temperament. Our lunch featured the sacramental of the one lonely fish caught. One brother had carefully packed wine and a makeshift chalice, hoping that the priest who came would think it wise to have Eucharist. Several hints throughout the day were made, but the priest's zeal for fishing matched the persistence of the would-be communicant. The elements finally returned to the monastery, slightly battered, but certainly unofficially sanctified. The futile fishing efforts extended to Hardscrabble Lake, existent beaver ponds, and several non-existent ones. We arrived at the monastery after bedtime, unheralded, ungreeted, and unacknowledged. Evidently the monastery had been hit by a sizable storm, with considerable water having seeped into the basement level. Unenthusiastic unpacking, a slow shower, and a somewhat feeble effort at supper closed the day. I found, somewhat surprisingly, a peaceful welcome in the solitariness of my cell. After a day of togetherness and conversation, two aspirins and the surrounding darkness of the night were rare blessings, fast becoming familiar friends.

Wednesday, August 2

Walking down the road to the eggery I gained insight into the Trappist vow of stability, i.e. commitment for life to one place. There is joy and wisdom in knowing thoroughly a particular piece of the earth with the same detailed knowledge one has of one's own hand—each flower and tree by name, the habits of each animal, the moods of the mountains and the seasons, reading wisely the weather, and growing old together with each part. There is enough mystery and excitement and suffering and joy in one acre of land to fill a person's whole life.

It was a mediocre day. So by chance I wandered for the first time into the music room, looking for one of my favorite records. There it was. It took only three bars for me to realize how deeply I missed not hearing music around. I laughed out loud, felt my eyes twinkle, started to sing, and danced all over the basement. It felt light, filling, intoxicating—I was in love, in ecstasy, in real joy over life and Being. Significantly, one of the songs was, "What You Learn in the Dark You Must Tell in the Light." It was only ten minutes. Then I went to the chapel. The words rolled out. It was genuine prayer.

Later I shared my experience with Br. "C," who is both cook and organist. "I understand," he said. "Up to six years ago, Trappists were not allowed to listen to music. But when that changed, I hiked to the Rock Point overlooking the monastery valley, and listened on a tape recorder to *Swan Lake*. We'll have to go there together."

This music experience was important. It seemed to show how, in the midst of things not going as one might hope, the recall and reorientation can come quickly, without effort. In fact, can it be that music itself is for me the ecstatic prayer of the mystic?

Thursday, August 3

Today I awoke with the clear awareness that if there is to be significant change, it must be at the wellsprings of mood and behavior—with one's scars. I carried a paper and pencil all day, letting my mind flow over the past, especially my early life, jotting down events, words, people, images—letting them come. I prayed for relaxed lack of defensiveness or fear. It was a James Joyce type of stream of consciousness, one thing evoking another for no known reason. I am not finished, of course, but it is a significant start. The sifting seemed to indicate my life as variations on the theme of acceptance, and the acts used to acquire or "deserve" it (grace and works). And these variations emerged as sub-themes:

1. The fear of being abandoned (and alone) and yet the yearning to be free—to belong and yet to be utterly independent and self-constituting.

2. The fear of rejection (from behavior to appearance), urging a need to earn acceptance through acceptability.

3. Fear of being done unto (of being made an object), leaving those scars which foster the development of power sufficient to establish one's rights and ultimately to fight for others who seem likewise to be on the outside—whether ethnic, sexual, or economic.

4. Sexuality (craving to be one with), forcing one outside oneself, sometimes "at any cost," daring one into vulnerability and venturing loss of self, in the longing for an almost transcendent unity.

5. God. Kant identified "God" as one regulative focus around which the mind yearns to organize and understand reality, yet is deprived of any experience of such reality. I see now that all of my life has been a craving for such unity, far surpassing the cool logic of my ordering mind. And once claimed, the passion shifts 180°, to the craving to behold all of life from the perspective of God. This is the meaning of having the mind of Christ. It is in this sense that I am branded to be a theologian.

What seems to be happening is a reseeing of my early life now through the eyes of grace—of acceptance and forgiveness. Freud is right in saying that repression into the unconscious occurs when the young, fledgling self cannot cope with the trauma in which it is involved. It denies it by pushing it out of sight, but literally not "out of mind." So it remains, for years, undealt with, but letting its unconscious presence be felt. Its presence may become more venturesome in the relaxed "carelessness" of sleep, but even here it remains largely hidden, in dream images.

But what of the relaxed presence of prayer recentered with the awareness of being totally accepted by God, as "heir," making unnecessary (rather than "wrong") the unsuccessful and often disastrous earlier behavior? Forgiveness is to relive by reseeing from different eyes. "They know not what they do." And so I began an extended process of "roving prayer." I resaw my early home. I visited each room, porch, yard. I let it tell its stories: the double house, isolated between boulevard and refinery, sulfur creek and abandoned factory, an only child aloneness, fearful of the huge venture of kindergarten across the boulevard and up the hill, of the uneasiness about "being left," wherever, and the night on the stairs, peering between the banisters to see if I was really alone, abandoned. I was.

I need more periods of this process of reconstituting by reliving. Call it confession and absolution, if one wants, but it is the process of intense reworking through the eyes of the Divine Companionship.

At lunch I become conscious of the uncharacteristically fast pace of monastic eating. I asked several monks. "I guess it comes from our long past of not being permitted to enjoy life. For ascetics, food is a necessary chore, to be done quickly and pragmatically." This seems to relate to Br. "C's" observation that Trappists were not permitted the love of things of beauty. It would seem that the post-Vatican II efforts to find monastic meaning in life together needs further expansion to affirm with simplicity their growing joy with and in creation.

Friday, August 4

I continued the process of prayer as reconstitution of memory, "finishing" my high school period. Standing around the altar at Eucharist, I found myself rising on my tiptoes. I remember looking several times at the Abbot who is a tall man, and thinking that we were of equal height. Toward the end of the Mass, the words "standing tall" embedded themselves in my mind. During the benediction I became aware of what was happening: what was being replaced by the prayer reprocessing, it seems, is the image I have had since a boy—that of being a "skinny runt." I was "becoming" tall, full, assured.

In preparation for a session with the Abbot, I summarized my experience thus far, identifying ten key happenings:

1. "Elisha"—through *lectio divina* the reclaiming of biblical material as shaping my own life and personality, helping me to regain my heritage.
2. "On the other side"—the "moment" of becoming free to speak as prayer.
3. "Abba repetition"—a way of practicing the presence.
4. "Centering prayer"—the "high" of resting in unity with the Ground of Being.
5. "Jesus prayer"—a method for so correlating prayer and bodily rhythm that "prayer without ceasing" becomes a life style.
6. "Musical joy"—an opening to "affective prayer" as the flowing of praise, simply for Being Itself.
7. "Healing scars"—transforming life by reopening and reliving. It is composed of two processes: (a) Stream of consciousness as a way of disclosing the hidden, noting clusters of "event periods." (b) Reliving such clusterings from the eyes of acceptance and forgiveness, until one is at peace sufficiently to close but not lock the door.
8. "Sexual craving"—that yearning for unity which in its insatiability, and indeed in its melancholy longing in the midst of its explicit expression, identifies this drive as spiritual. It is a luring foretaste, and the spiritual life radiates with its energy.
9. "Companion consciousness"—disciplined replacement of the I-me relationship which is consciousness with the ongoing I-Thou dialogue of transformed consciousness.
10. "Creative providence"—transforming morality by replacing the image of obedience to the prior will (law) of God with the companionship of mutual discovery. Instead of a human guessing game of the Divine requirements, the image is that of co-artists, shaping the

possible in the here and now, living on the yearning edge of the present as promise, in beauty.

The Abbot's response was encouraging. He suggested that what I was doing and what Ira Progoff was about were sufficiently related that I might want to scan his *At a Journal Workshop* for supporting context. I spoke to him about Zen meditation, which evidently is what is presently feeding him. They have had several Zen retreats at the monastery. "Several chapters in Merton's *Mystics and Zen Masters* will help you see that in the prayer of centering, something of Zen has already been begun."

Our session confirmed my growing awareness that only by creating sufficient discipline to filter our senses from surrounding bombardments will we be able to select the life that shall define us.

Although I was not present, I understand that at twilight our deer friend introduced her new family of two fawns to the community. I read with some nostalgia of three families who have been living for several years on land that is on permanent loan from the monks in Gethsemani, Kentucky. They live in simplicity as an alternative to contemporary culture, a kind of spiritual earthiness of survival and of "willing one thing." Deep pulling on my deep.

Saturday, August 5

A hard day. Worked with the Abbot in moving a heavy "buck-and-rider" fence to the archway of the monastery entrance. An artist woman from Aspen who designed the routed wood signs to replace the temporary ones came to supervise the staining. There is a fascinating dynamic when a woman comes into this male world. Each monk responded differently, but in each case there was an energy of needed response, by both.

This triggered more thinking about the issue of sexism in

Christianity. There has been heaviness in my awareness that early matriarchy as historic fact makes it impossible for us to justify the double standards of Christianity as primitive vestiges to be slowly educated out of the race. Nor can demythologizing be the answer, for it forfeits the Christian faith in history as the plane of God's activity. The answer may well be to take seriously the role of redactors in scriptural history. Meaning was first expressed orally, and only many years later written down; and still later these various writings were edited by "redactors" into theological wholes. Thus the Deuteronomic redactors' rerendering of the Israelite story into variations on the theme of law, reward, and punishment is paralleled by the vastly contrasting editing in each of the Gospels. Thus Scripture-tradition must be hyphenated, for just as Scripture resulted from tradition, so Scripture in turn is interpreted from some tradition. If one reads Christianity through the sexist eyes of many existing traditions, it must be rejected. But today, standing around the eucharistic table, I experienced again this act of eating and drinking as the interpenetration of lives with the Divine penetration of humanity in a new organic wholeness. It is from this promise that one may reimage the whole sordid Judaeo-Christian history, as at Emmaus all became clear in the breaking of bread.

Perhaps the total maleness (at its best) of the Trappist community helps illuminate the fascination of this community for Mary, the "Mother of God," the "Queen of heaven." In practice, it would seem, she and God the Son are the Divine Consorts imaging together for faith the nature of God, in spite of all rationality. Together there emerges Divinity as androgynous.

The Abbot asked if I would do the homily at a Sunday Mass before I left. I will want to respond, of course, to the Scripture of the day, but I will not be surprised if through my eyes that Scripture, whatever it is, will have something to say about the monastery in particular and the contemplative in general, as quietly subversive in the midst of an unsuspecting culture. We will see.

Sunday, August 6

I spent the early morning reading Merton on Zen. His interpretation resembles very much the theology of Paul Tillich. The Zen discipline to accomplish negation of the ego is akin to Tillich's "ontic shock." And the positive result, that of receiving a new self which gazes out, in, and through all things, is akin to Tillich's "transparency" or sacramental principle. Merton meaningfully quotes Rilke's poetry, contrasting spectatorship (conscious *of* or looking *at*) with looking *from* (outgazing), conscious *for* all of creation.

The homily today contained a helpful story. After the painter Monet died, the waterlily ponds at his home, the inspiration for some of his greatest paintings, were left to deteriorate. Lately they have been restored. An admirer of Monet who expectantly visited them left in bitter disappointment. The reason, it was suggested, is that the beauty could be beheld only through the vision of the artist. And so for the Christian. The reality is indeed in the eye of the beholder whose sensitivity is honed by and in the Eucharistic community.

For lunch we had mashed potatoes, gravy, and Copeland's *Appalachian Spring*—an unbeatable combination.

While I was ministering to the chickens, the Abbot announced during None the message just received through a long distance call—the Pope had died. I knew nothing of it until our picnic supper. There was a casual reference to the Pope's death. I thought they were teasing because of my negative estimate of Pope Paul's leadership. I had to get four independent verifications before I accepted it as true. Frankly, I was relieved, but the candidates do not seem overly promising.

There is something joyous about this place. The Abbot, prior, and a number of us stood in the parking lot of the monastery after returning from the ranch house, celebrating the "great silence" by laughing like little kids. Everything seemed fun. And only then did I discover the meaning of voices I heard the night before, especially one thundering voice that had said, "I guess we're in trouble because I just can't find it." I had visions of another broken water main with the turnoff valve being "undiscoverable." The truth, it turned out, was that a visitor had a set of golf clubs in his car; a few of the monks became sufficiently nostalgic to drive a few balls into the moonlit sagebrush.

Monday, August 7

They Speak By Silence reflects well the Carthusian spirituality, of which two points are worth remembering: (1) The great difference between faith and feeling. The latter, which might be peace or joy, is an added gift by God, given but usually taken away. What links the plateaus of feeling together is the determined faithfulness to believe nevertheless, and perhaps even more commonly, in spite of. (2) Prayer, in the end, is God praying in and through us.

Evelyn Underhill provided her own insightful summary of her long spirit life with the conclusion that prayer is at its best not praying in extended periods but in offering our wills to God throughout the day with "little darts of prayer."

Just before Eucharist I came upon a powerful set of lines in T. S. Eliot. After four *Preludes* in which the images of poverty, boredom, and abandonment in the cities are overwhelming, he is moved by fancies curled around this image: "The notion of some infinitely gentle/Infinitely suffering thing."

There was a Mass in honor of Pope Paul. The visiting monk who yesterday scorned *Appalachian Spring* as music "best sold by the yard" was the celebrant. He declared Pope Paul as near an incarnation of the Beatitudes as it is possible in this life to get. During intercessions one of our monks prayed that Paul's successor "would be one who would continue the policies established by Paul and further unfalteringly his interpretation of the implications of the faith." I cringed physically. The sparseness of "amens" gave me solace that I did not stand alone. I was brought to greater awareness of the miracle of the church. When one considers the political, cultural, personal infighting surrounding the key events that have defined the Church's life, it is miraculous that the major decisions have been so faithful. I am thinking particularly of such events as Nicaea, or Chalcedon, or Vatican II. As one brother put it, "Somehow the Church manages to blunder through, but it won't make the same mistake twice." Despite its hypocrisy and ponderous irrelevancy at times, the power of the channel markers of tradition remains irreplaceable, especially as this is incarnated in liturgy. The task, it seems, is not so much the relevantly new as the rediscovery of the profoundly old, as if for the first time, in creative faithfulness.

Referring to the picnic the day before, I whispered at lunch to the Abbot, "You sure know how to throw a swell party." Without missing a beat, he replied, "Thanks, you sure know how to be a good loser." He was referring, unfortunately, to the accompanying volleyball game.

Tuesday, August 8

The Communion solo illustrated the tendency to squander the objective givenness of tradition in a sloppy kind of subjective theological reversal. It had something to do with sailing beyond the seas, and whoever smells a rose knows Christ. And most revealing, "He who sees man sees God." If the good news is the God-like quality of the human species readily recognizable, I'll vote for Satan.

It was an enjoyable day—working with wood and my hands. I secured a banister that had been loose for years, and began building an egg shelf for the processing "department," one that can be swung out of the way to load cartons.

Wednesday, August 9

I was very tired, and after studying for two hours this morning I went back to bed. It was thoroughly delightful in a new way. I began with meditating, which mellowed into a short sleep, from which I awoke with words of thanks, which in being savored filtered down deeply into a floating half-sleep of being grounded and supported, awakening in a kind of happiness. I was swept by this rhythm a number of times and arose very rested and newly appreciative of life.

The daily office is arranged here in such a way that we sing each psalm once in a two-week period. The psalms are truly the hymn book of the Christian faith, and certainly the center of Jesus' life of prayer. Recently, however, I had experienced the psalms as being increasingly foreign, theologically. My image was of a theology stressing obedience of the law and the consequent reward, or lamenting the way things are until it becomes revealed that the wicked will get punished in the end after all. Such simplism is neither satisfying nor accurate. So I began studying the psalms, taking them slowly in groups of five. Although I have not finished, the contrast from my stereotype of them is striking. They are honest in questioning God. They are not at all sure that reward-punishment is the way things work; and in the end the psalmist hopes against hope and has faith often with little evidence that God is ultimately in control. They are refreshingly straightforward in their feelings of anger and hatred. I arbitrarily chose a psalm and began listing some of the key words—rebuke, groaning, anguish, death, abandoned, weeping, wasting, grief, weak, foes, evil, ashamed, troubled, pray, deliver. These are truly the songs of the earth and the searchings of the human heart. Somehow it is all there.

Today one could sense an uneasiness in the community. The "family doctor" of the monastery has asked to meet with the monks tonight to discuss their diet and eating practices. He will be bringing with him a nutritionist. Ironically, we just received an expensive carrot crusher as one of the latest of the apparatuses for simplicity. It will be interesting to see what happens. Rumor has it that in a recent physical the Abbot was found lacking in sodium and was told to sin gracefully by using salt.

Thursday, August 10

As I think back over the long night with the doctor and nutritionist, it seems that I have experienced another possible "breakthrough." It was a bit unfair, however, as the nutritionist turned out to be a beautiful sun-tanned woman, so obviously healthy that one was tempted to be an instant believer, even before hearing the subject. The Abbot, it turned out, was found not only deficient in sodium (related to absence of salt) but also calcium. It seems that in installing a distiller in the name of better health, the natural water here which is high in minerals is having removed the very content which is essential to health. The basic importance of the session was the clear, commonsense, documented manner in which good eating was presented as essential to rhythmic life. Medicines, in many ways, are the artificial way of dealing with the disruptions of the body caused by the artificial food which has made our bodies more machines than living organisms. Particularly powerful for the monks in their task of raising chickens (as over against producing eggs) was the disclosure that supermarket eggs are produced by chickens in a totally artificial environment, given "speed" to hop them up to produce more eggs than their bodies are created to lay. This so weakens the chickens that their food has to contain antibiotics; and their bodies, no longer being able to fight off lice, etc., need to be artificially sprayed. The result is artificial eggs containing foreign ingredients; and when the chickens are sold for soup, the resulting product contains contaminating amounts of poisons. In illustration after illustration, the doctor and the nutritionist documented the image of food as no longer for health, for the liturgical act of meaningful consumption, but the creation of products serving profit and the economy, indifferent to the person, except as seducible purchaser. Quantity has suffocated quality. And this dynamic is irreversible, given the economic "value" informing this culture. Thus, just as the Trappist reorders the external environment as a citadel of silence for the soul, it follows that he must develop a self-conscious discipline of consumption if the soul-body organism is not to be unknowingly subverted. Key words used during the session were: natural, moderation, non-artificial, non-additives, assortment (allergies usually result from the ongoing eating of the same thing), minerals (more important than vitamins), minimum cooking, fasting (a natural cleansing, especially if done with an assortment of natural juices), order (e.g. the order of eating should be protein, carbohydrates, salad, and, later, fruit).

They thought that the monastic eggs were excellent, except for two things—the need for exposure by the chickens to sun, and the need for the eggs to be fertilized (this, evidently, reduces the cholesterol). It is interesting that while the raising of chickens began here simply as a means of economic survival, it could well become a symbolic mission: distilling the Trappist spirituality into the care of an egg, the traditional symbol of resurrection and new life.

I was moved by the fact that when it did not seem that I would be invited to the nutritional meeting, several monks expressed disappointment. One monk asked what questions I wanted asked, and another volunteered to take notes.

Today was the feast of Br. Lawrence (third century). As a young man he was in charge of the papal treasury. When the Roman persecution sentenced the Pope to execution, the emperor ordered that the wealth of the Church be given to him. Lawrence asked for three days to get it ready. Then he distributed the whole of the treasury to the poor, and on the third day he gathered the poor in a church, inviting the emperor to come and see the church's "true wealth." Lawrence was roasted over a fire until dead, yet with such a spirit that he advised his tormentors on how best to do a roast "well-done."

Friday, August 11

In a tape on meditation played during lunch, there was reference made to W. H. Auden's idea that the university should become a secular environment of meditation. That is, it must teach selfless concentration on that which is immediately before one, whether a microscope slide, a poem, or a mathematical problem. This recalled for me a story told of Martin Buber whose earlier thought centered in the idea of transparency, i.e., in seeing the depths *through* whatever was before him. One day a student, after visiting him, committed suicide. From then on, Buber's thought shifted significantly to intense concentration on whatever was before him, in which the "other" was no longer transparent but incarnational. Dialogue became the primary mode of knowing and being. It is rare today when any person is totally available to another, without preoccupation, concern to have one's own say, or desire for reorientating the conversation to oneself. Yet such undivided and undistracted presence is salvific, revelatory of the Divine presence, for without the latter the former is impossible. The loss of self *for* the other by being *in* the other is *the* form of spirituality. This seems to be one of the significant insights of my stay here.

Saturday, August 12

My work task was to transplant more wild grass as sod in the garth. Br. "H" was leveling the parking lot with the backhoe. We looked at each other, at the tediousness of the transplanting process, and at almost the same moment responded, "Why not?" So we did. A bit absurd, but we planted grass with a huge backhoe. I can't say it came out too level or even that we got the pieces of "sod" exactly where we wanted. But we had a good time laughing, and who knows? In the years to come nature might do wonders with our work.

A letter was waiting from one of our highest graduating seminarians last year. It exemplified well the agony of the Gospel, the craving that grounds the Christian's pilgrimage, and the insatiability that discerns everything else but God as insufficient. "My life has been miserable since we left Missouri (he is beginning Ph.D. work). Nothing seems to help. I have tried reading (Bible, O'Neill, Warren, Updike, Lessing, Shelley, Barth, et al.; not even Hopkins has helped), drinking (mostly

Rolling Rock Beer from Pa.), praying, talking, writing letters, listening to records (Joplin, Bach, Ravel, etc.), even studying Greek. I feel lost or misbegotten or dreamless or homesick or something. Other than a doctor with socialist tendencies who diagnosed my phlebitis at a free clinic, I have met only one person I can talk to—he is a beginning seminary student, a sixties' liberal. I'm still lonely. No one really to talk to about how I synthesize Barth and Marx; Hopkins and Thomas; prayer and swearing; Bach and Ravel (even you don't understand that one); existentialism and dogmatics. But I'm not convinced my real problem is communal—it is still cosmic/comic. I'm estranged from me, God, all. I don't have an anchor, nothing is sure. I know it is all promise, appetite, abstraction. But I am weary in the wilderness—manna sucks. Meaning must be more substantial than promise can possibly be. I'm a vapor in the wind. It seems God is blowing me around, while what I want is for God to suck me into Herself . . . I wish I could discover how I really want to spend these fleeting days in an earthen vessel. I want to be something—happy, fulfilled, consummated, dead? No, not dead. I want to be alive and I feel dead. Maybe I should run for Pope . . . I hope you got religion there at the monkery and that you share it with me. I doubt if religion/faith can be shared at all. It's probably sort of a gift or something. I got just enough to make me miserable . . ." Perhaps I should have worried, or had regrets, or sorrow, or something negative. But I celebrated. He has been bitten; he is experiencing what Eliot called "Christ the tiger" or Simone Weil termed "God's terrible love" or what Merton meant by "the burned men." He is on the way to detachment, emptiness, a kind of giving up. He may never know the other side; but one thing is sure—there is no other way *to* the other side than through what he is experiencing.

I feel this so deeply, yet I am perplexed recently by Carol Ochs (*Behind the Sex of God*). For her, Patriarchy chooses exile and wandering, in estrangement from this world, as pilgrims. Matriarchy nurtures those who feel at home in this world, who put down roots. Faber sees these contrasts as two types of persons, largely set by one's earliest years—those at home in the

121

world, where they belong and where they can trust; and those who are the unwanted, the aliens, those in but not of this world. Soelle speaks most to me, for while she (as I) is most sensitive to lack as the roots of spirituality, she too seems to dwell in the antinomy of knowing both to be so: the creation that in its tragedies and ecstasies feeds the craving for the mysteriously wholly other, and the God who in turn has become incarnate in that very cosmos, as the home of his promised co-creative vision of consummation, in joyously agonizing foretaste now.

In planning the work for my remaining time, I suggested to Br. "A" that the "cemetery" is, so to speak, dying. We took a walk in that direction to see. After several false starts we found it among the sagebrush. How quickly things return from whence they came. The question was a kind of parable: How does one respect the natural rhythms and still respond creatively with a touch of promise. My guess is that when I leave, the sagebrush will still be winning, 2 to 1.

Sunday, August 13

During the early hours I experienced an approach to prayer that could be increasingly meaningful. It could be called image flow. It begins as a prayer of centering, but instead of controlling the mental images with a mantra, one invites them to "do their thing"—a kind of free floating, associational image show. One "watches," not regulating, or interpreting, or analyzing, or even feeling—one just let's the process be/become. It is like dreaming, only one is far more attentive to "what is going on," to the surfacing of the interfacings of self. Before one is through, one may be impacted by joy, or fear, or struggle, or anxiety, or the problematic—but whatever, the self is knowing itself now by relaxing in its presence. One may then just let it be with satisfaction, or some "doing" may be required.

At Communion, I found myself fascinated by the face of each person as he came forward. Suffering, joy, agony, searching—in each face—the lines, twinkle, beaten posture, lively step, upturned tentativeness. I was awed by the depth, the incomprehensibility, the bottomlessness of it all. Everything, right here, infinite mystery—material only for the mystic or the poet. By seeing each face as if it were the only one, each took on a uniquely particular beauty. I couldn't find it for each person, but for more than I had imagined. It seemed related to whether a person seemed to take himself with something of the same seriousness with which I was trying to see him. This may be what it means to see each person as the one for whom Christ died.

Monday, August 14

It is becoming clearer how one's personal pilgrimage is one with the social pilgrimage. Whether one talks of diet, community, transformed consciousness, presence, providence, vision, or death, in all of these one stands over against this culture. Just to "do one's thing" is a kind of warfare for the elbow room in which to be; and integrity seems to demand that one likewise create the holy space and time for others to be. One reason why so many of us who are "fugitives" of the 1960's are frustrated is because of such little success. That is why the pilgrimage of Spirit is so necessary, as a depth grounding rather than a retreat. Only then can we understand how profoundly right Barth was when he said that success is not in our hands; our task is to be faithful. It was perhaps parabolic that in the midst of this meditation I felt compelled to write a letter to a friend in struggle over life directions, and found that the writing was a continuation of the meditation, in no way a disruption or diversion.

Tuesday, August 15

Surprisingly we had a heavy night rain which by morning gifted us with icy boardwalks, frosted grass, and snow on the mountains. With temperatures in the 20's and jackets hurriedly rediscovered, each of us was separately drawn outside into the rhythm of change. It was sensed as a harbinger for autumn's exciting sadness.

For the first time, I moved into the "big time." I was named one of the "officers" of the week—reader during lunch. The book is Louis Lekai's *The Cistercians: Ideals and Reality.* But since today is the feast of Mary's Assumption, music was played instead. Although the choice of Strauss waltzes struck me at first as at least weird, the more I listened to the light flights of emotional, happy fantasy, the more appropriate it seemed to be. A reading from Rahner the night before at Vespers identified the mood, suggesting Mary to be the first to participate in the resurrection promised *bodily* to the faithful.

It is strange and interesting that in a place supposedly remote and solitary, the monastery is "found" by so many in a way that makes for creative traffic. When one retreats from the world, the world has a way of seeking one out. During the next several days, Br. David Steindl-Rast will be with us. He is a Benedictine hermit from Connecticut, originally from Austria, who is an excellent writer, understands and knew Merton well, and, unlike Merton, has experienced Zen through at least three years in one of their monasteries.

While the other monks picnicked with the Abbot's family, David and I climbed to the top of the hill behind the monastery. Astride the majestic vantage point of the water tower we watched the sun go down and spoke of life and death. A beautiful time, rare, close. The theme of Mary was raised again, in two different ways. The first was the Christian response as absurdity in the face of death's absurdity—to dance at the funeral, and play Strauss in the face of death's finality. I shared with him Dylan Thomas' response of raging in the face of death's darkness: "Do not go gentle into that good night . . ." And he shared with me Edna St. Vincent Millay's "Dirge Without Music":

Quietly they go, the intelligent, the witty, the brave.
I know. But I do not approve. And I am not resigned.

We discussed Mariology in the Church's history as having aris-
en largely in reaction to the dominance of a one-sided maleness
of God. As the feminine quality of God is increasingly claimed,
the need for such a dominant place for Mary will diminish.

We returned to the monastery expecting to prepare a very
simple supper and create Vespers together. But in the midst of
our supper preparations, the monks returned for Vespers. Vespers we had, but supper we had not. Nevertheless I went to bed
feeling richly fed.

Wednesday, August 16

I found interesting a letter from a friend.

I hope you are really learning to "waste" time, to just
sit and *be* without *doing* anything, to give up control (of
yourself). Your sensitivity for feeling so rich and full,
with music, sexuality, touch, joy, etc., are feelings I've
hoped for you. There's something so valuable about
tasting that simplicity, even once. It will stay with
you—i.e. the capacity will be with you ...

I worked alone this morning, repairing the large barn doors. It
felt very good: sun, quiet, brute heaviness, the useful.

Our guest, Br. David, asked if we could spend more time together. He and the Abbot are going to a religious commune near
Taos that is presently without religious leadership. Its effort is
at religious pluralism, with its minimal exposure being to Christianity. What will come of the ten days is not clear, but I sense
in David and the Abbot, as I did in Merton and many other monastic types, an openness, indeed a longing, to be in relationship
with non-Christian spirituality. It is as if the contemplative experience and even its "techniques" transcend all conceptual interpretations, and in the face of the non-contemplative nature of
modern society, spiritualities have more in common than in difference.

Perhaps "sensitivity" characterizes the new emerging monastic life style. David and I sense this in each other, despite heavy differences in personality. In fact, being with him helped me identify myself as a "dialectic" person—I characteristically define something in terms of what it is not, in terms of contrast. And only later, sometimes only as eschatological promise, do I sense the synthesis. David is "irenic"—he senses the commonality immediately and admits difference only later and often grudgingly. This may be a difference between activist and contemplative, yet in my relation with David it is clear that we come from a common experience and sensitivity. Perhaps the difference is the one Schlesinger noted in the Kennedy brothers: "One attacked injustices because he found them irrational, the other because he found them unbearable." We exchanged favorite book titles—his for me were from Rilke, Watts and Dodd; mine for him were from Barth, Niebuhr, Cullmann, and Miguez-Bonino.

In the afternoon three of us were told to prepare the refectory for a concert tonight. The Juilliard String Quartet, it seems, has found us out.

While we were working, a lay person who identified himself as a "conscientious Catholic" dropped by to "chat." After a while he related his hassle with the zoning commission of the town to which he was moving his business. He informed us with delight that he had found a "real steal"—a furnished house for $1,400.00 a month. I felt a deep coldness gnawing at me. Where I live many are fortunate to *make* $300 a month. Can we be part of the same Gospel, when there is in me the persistent trust, rooted in the promise of the Gospel, concerning the reversal of first and last? The Gospel is good news directly only for the empty. Yet the monks seemed genuine in their affirmation of his "good fortune." In the deep aloneness that I felt, I suddenly was swept with how deeply the wrenching going on in my deepest soul matched the inner but largely unspoken creativity of this place. I, who have been so intimately involved in the social apostolate, drawn in pursuit of something I know not what in the midst of those who through the centuries have been

126

so traditionally and "notoriously" withdrawn from all of this. And at the same time it is here, in the very midst of such contemplation and silence that I experience the thundering of the God of the "still small voice" that forces the monks beyond themselves. It is incredible, but my journey outward has wrested me inward; and their pilgrimage inward is compelling them outward, perhaps as much against their will as is my unwanted journey. T. S. Eliot's words were reborn: "the way up is the way down, the way forward is the way back." In a deep and mutual confession by letter months later, the Abbot was to say:

"During the past 6–8 years we have come to realize that we can no longer take a position of withdrawal and unconcern toward the world beyond the walls of the monastery. We believe that even though we are not 'of the world,' we are still 'in the world,' and part of that world, and that our lifestyle and actions are critical and somehow instrumental in bringing about or retarding the Kingdom of God, that justice and peace are as much our responsibility as those who have expressly dedicated their lives to this purpose. We have experienced the need to rethink our traditional structures in the light of this shift of consciousness and to be able to move in this direction, but without losing the vital contemplative dimension which, we believe, is our first contribution to the Church and to society. The movement has been slow and clumsy in coming, as you witnessed; however the movement and the struggle which it entails is with us."

But at this particular moment I could only sense dimly what before I left I prayed I would come to understand—that the depths are the heights, and that in is out, and the way of silence entails considerable sound, and that radical social change must originate in emptiness, and that the resurrection of this nation is at the intersections which are crucifixion. Somehow it is all one, and the Kingdom is the ache of such dissonance for the consonant which transcends by invading. Too much.

Such struggle seemed acted out as we worked hard to turn the refectory into a context for beauty. One could sense the excitement. We moved in benches to make seating for fifty—for the musicians' friends, and for folks living near the monastery.

In the process of preparations Br. "C" invented a new recipe for toll house cookies. All afternoon he fantasized and strategized about selling it to the chocolate company to make millions for the poor. With coffee, tea, and four gallons of lemonade, things were nervously ready for our big debut. The quartet was dressed very informally. It was the first time that I had seen women in any part of the monastery other than the chapel—it was almost like open house. The introductory remarks set the mood: "This is no concert. Rather it is like being in our living room, and the four of us are going to make music, for you but above all for us." Throughout the Haydn, Bach and Beethoven they would talk to each other, trying new rhythms, responding to their moods together. Delightful. The informality afterward was likewise a process of surprises. One guest was an operatic soloist from New York who had been singing in Aspen. Another was a Greek Orthodox librarian from Aspen High School. I took the risk of showing her our library, only to be "discovered" several minutes later by the Abbot who feigned an "off-limits scowl," followed by an equally feigned "that's OK tonight" smile. People left slowly until only the community remained. Two of us who were "residents" restored order while the rest stood around gradually unwinding, their task being, evidently, the elimination of all remaining cookies and lemonade. They took to their "mission" with persistent intensity. By 10:30, with the excitement of little children permitted on Christmas Eve to stay up far beyond their bedtime, we debated the rising hour and went happily to bed.

Thursday, August 17

Today Br. "B" came home from the hospital after minor surgery on his knee. One could tell how pleased he was to be home again. When I brought his luncheon tray to his cell he kept laughing with a kind of giggle—a delighted chuckle of being loved by his family.

There was a picnic at the Ranch House for Fr. "E's" family.

I decided not to go, although I was made to feel quite welcome and thoroughly missed. I was aware that I would leave in two weeks, and my solitude was a bit off-center from activity. I sensed in myself that the taste for quiet was becoming sufficiently deep as a disciplined priority, even in the face of volleyball and picnics. It felt good quietly just to be.

From various quarters the news filtered in to prepare for a snowstorm moving in from Wyoming. With temperatures in the 70's it was hard to believe, but the snow several days before made it more plausible. Again, one could sense excitement over the "little" things.

Friday, August 18

The snow didn't come, but the monastery was ascetically and shiveringly cold. I worked outside most of the morning—cold, crisp, leaf burning weather. I finished the morning by building a bench under the aspen trees. The hermit happened by about that time, and so together we sat, consecrating the bench relatedly to the glory of God and the doing of nothing. He talked of solitude as a way of standing up to ultimate questions and (to use his favorite phrase) "going for it." We promised that from now on this bench would recall where two friends sat and enjoyed each other. The twinkle in his eyes showed a rare pleasure at that. We parted with a question: "Can a person be a hermit and 'do nothing' without being overcome by guilt, especially by seeing the work that others have to do for him?" We smiled. There was no answer.

For lunch we played Vivaldi's *Four Seasons*, beginning with "Fall" and going into "Winter." The wind outside assumed the viola part. Melancholy, subdued, simple, brown-like. Fr. "F" came late as the meal was almost over, so when the others left we shared the melodic anticipation captured in the winter movement. That afternoon the two of us finished our jobs a little early. On the basis of spontaneous inspiration (Holy Spirit or otherwise), we went down to the pasture, "captured" two horses, and rode off onto the high mesa. It was glorious—crisp, cloud-shrouded peaks, irrigated fields, wind in the tall grass. There was a special specialness in the fact that, having almost never ridden a horse, I knew little about shifting gears and even less about the brake.

When I returned to my cell, I realized how unread were most of the books I had brought. Somehow, for the first time in years, it did not matter.

When I got to the kitchen, the prior was suggesting a big fish fry a week from Sunday as a farewell for Fr. "F" and me. Fr. "F" is returning to his own monastery after four months "on loan." He was excited, and immediately began a fantasy concerning the types of ice cream and cake he preferred. I had more a touch of sadness.

Saturday, August 19

This morning was a full moon vigil, complete with coyote chorus. About 6:00 A.M. I started for breakfast, got as far as the cloister, and audibly gasped. The red ridge which is an extension of "Silver Mountain" was aglow with the pink reflection of the sunrise, and perched as a golden ball right above her was the moon, total and complete. What a breathless, beautiful, helpless feeling. One can only stare and make some quiet weird noise. Other monks were doing the same—just looking.

In gathering the trash, I was told to remove the garbage can at the steps from the visitors' parking lot. Long has it been the trusty refuge for stray wrappers, bubble gum, and cigarette butts as one mounted the steps to the guest chapel, "unburdened." As I stored it in the far corner of the barn, it seemed that I was quietly marking the end of an era.

The rest of the work period was, at my initiative, in the cemetery. Sagebrush had reclaimed the path, and ground squirrels had set up residency on one of the graves, unceremoniously in the neighborhood of the deceased's belly-button. There was something whole and earthy about working there, on one's hands and knees, sawing the sagebrush—touching, smelling, seeing, hearing, even tasting. At mid-afternoon, with shovel attached, I was called down to meet five youthful women who came to plan and practice a liturgical dance for tomorrow's liturgy. Their somewhat sheer, low, pure white flowing dresses, and bare feet, seemed in stark contrast with at least the austere brick and tile chapel. Their theme was from Beethoven's life—the movement from despair over his growing deafness to the choice in spite of it to persevere. Out of this decision came some of his greatest music. Fr. "E" suggested slyly that this was the theme of crucifixion and resurrection. And I, hopefully seeking support for my homily, offered the theme of emptiness for fullness. They will dance immediately following the distribution of Communion. By the time they had rehearsed twice in that space, the movement had become gracefully liturgical.

Fr. "E" will be celebrant tomorrow—in addition to the homily, he asked me to read the Gospel and lead the prayers of the faithful. I experienced tears when he gave me his own cowl to wear. How to put it on gracefully must remain one of the best kept mysteries in Christendom. I was amazed by the sleeves, extending almost to one's knees. The only explanation I got was: "That's traditional."

Sunday, August 20

It is early morning. I have prepared the homily the best I know how. I can only prayfully wait. This is a very different experience for me because of the context. If I am able to communicate well, it will be to say that these monks in this place are subversives, not so much because of what they say or even think, but what they are, often unknowingly or against their will. But such subversion is contagious. In the midst of a culture of noise, these little white-robed men who like to play with bells choose silence; in a culture of work, they choose contemplation; in a culture of self-realization, they renounce the self; in a culture of achievement, they declare that the winner will be a loser, and

131

only the loser a winner; in a culture whose economy is utterly dependent on consumption, they insist on emptiness; in a culture structured by possession, they insist upon detachment; in a culture intoxicated with facts and education, they insist on ignorance as the basis of wisdom; in a culture of complexity they call us to the simplicity of willing one thing; in a culture intent on a high standard of living they insist on a high standard of life. Achievement versus grace; the exposure of the emptiness of fullness for the sake of the fullness of emptiness. The heart of this subversion is in planting within a person the appetite for silence. And once planted, once one tastes silence, and listening, and stopping, and being flooded by a Depth beyond all words, once one lets go so that one's hands are empty for the first time, once you do nothing, say nothing, think nothing, but just let yourself *be* in the midst of Capital Peak or a columbine or Snowmass Creek or the mist of a morning valley—if you ever let it happen, it is all over for you. From then on, everything else seems insane. It begins with doing nothing and not feeling guilty. And out of it comes the awareness of what Pascal called "the God-shaped vacuum in each of us," the craving homesickness for a place where one has never been before. This is the restlessness that Augustine knew, that nothing in this culture can ever fill. Then one lives in active waiting, for to do anything yet is for the wrong end, with the wrong motive, to wait with detachment in the emptiness. I plan to end with "helpful suggestions" for escaping such subversion, such as watching TV for three hours a day, or carrying a transistor radio with extra batteries, or joining everything in sight—but never, never letting oneself be alone in the silence with oneself. And I will end as I began, with a warning: that those present are in the midst of a very subversive place, with subversive people, nestled in subversive mountains with subversive streams and extremely subversive wildflowers. May somehow the message be heard.

It is now evening. I believe I was heard. My gift was a surprise visit by my oldest daughter and her husband. So, complete with peanut butter and jelly sandwiches, we hiked above cow camp and experienced Capital Peak from the beaver ponds. It is a special place.

At the weekly evening discussion supper the conversation turned to the Trappist way of death. It centers in the simplicity of returning a brother to the earth, clothed in his cowl. He is lowered with straps, without coffin or even a box, and gently covered with earth, beginning with the feet, and finally the head. Each set of monks in turn participates in the finality by personally doing some of the shoveling. In all of this there was a refreshing willingness to talk of death without morbidity or apparent fear or uneasiness. In fact gentle and spontaneous humor seemed appropriate.

Monday, August 21

While processing eggs, the prior shared with me training sessions they have had over the years, such as Zen retreats, a Progoff Intensive Journal workshop, Yoga training, diet sessions, E.S.T. value training, and six Rolfing sessions for each monk. The impression conveyed was that of pluralism, a deep respect for the views of others, and a sensitivity to the individual needs of each monk. Inflexibility, defensiveness, and unwillingness to change seem to be the primary "sins."

Around 5:00 P.M. we had a rare visitation. I was meditating at my desk when onto the garth walked a deer, quietly but with calm assurance. In a moment a fawn followed, and then, as though that were not enough, a second fawn joined the parade. I was overwhelmed; my only reaction was to want to share it. I got Br. "B", and he hobbled into my cell, as excited as I. Some of the monks were upstairs, so we called them on the phone. The deer went behind the evergreens, which put them within two feet of the huge windows in the cloister. All of us stood transfixed, in a strangely mutual and awesome eye dialogue. The fawns wandered off, but the mother stayed. As I watched later from my cell, she wandered toward my window, dandelion plant to dandelion plant, until I heard her breathing and could have touched her from my open window. I was entranced. She had marvelously huge ears, attentive in direction to every sound; she was plagued with insects, particularly around the eyes, using her ears to chase them. How gently and artfully she scratched her head with the hoof of the back left leg. And then, as in all things it seems, a conflict of values set in. She eyed the small aspen trees that we had been so lovingly cultivating all summer. And, with delicate but determined gulps, the trees began vanishing, one by one. I could not bring myself to say "no," and the "yes" likewise was beyond me. She stayed for several hours, until the bell for Vespers became her call to walk into the sunset.

If a monk came to make supper who had not yet met the deer, he was personally escorted out for an introduction. Ironically, this process exacerbated an old wound concerning the issue of silence. Appeal was hastily made to the prior: "Can we or can we not talk in the kitchen?" "A good question," was his reply. Since it had been made plain that I was to maintain silence and eat in the refectory, that was where I went, not passing "Go." The sound of argument persisted. One can obey an inflexible rule—but confusion results when there are exceptions and the logic of the exceptions is unclear or non-existent. The appearance is that of double standard: silence for others, exceptions for oneself. This is particularly difficult for a resident or novice, who must simply "take it" and learn much about human nature. The frictions of community, it would seem, cluster not so much around important issues as with daily "trivia," ranging from toothpaste squeezing to dishwashing "technique." To be, it seems, is naturally to assume that one's own norms are the norms for being as such.

Tuesday, August 22

In a little over one week I will be leaving. I have very contradictory feelings: I wish it would come quickly and be done with; I hope it never comes. I recall the story told of St. Francis who, as he was hoeing his garden, was asked, "What would you do if you knew that you would die today?" He replied, "I would hoe my garden." So, should I spend my last week as all my others here? Or should it be special, assimilating and putting things into perspective? But what of these three months would I want to render indelible? Perhaps it is "companionship," signaled for me by the very capacity for prayer, for prayer as affective conversation is becoming increasingly natural. Before such flowing is swallowed up in a daily inner city sameness, I need to taste it as deeply as possible. Yet relationship with God must rest on that objectivity that only faith can affirm. Faith is risking in spite of much that one has experienced, and disciplining one's life to that commitment. Subjective experience may come as a gift, but it is sporadic at best, *and is no foundation for prayer.* Long ago I learned this from deep human relations; they rest ultimately not on love but on promise, for promise alone can string the gifts of experience into a meaningful whole. As Barth put it, "Whoso means to rescue and preserve the subjective element shall lose it; but whoso gives it up for the sake of the objective shall save it." To live one's life disciplined to the Divine promise of companionship.

So? Perhaps a final retreat of total silence at the hermitage? Or is that just one final last-ditch effort at self-control rather than abandonment?

Wednesday, August 23

In discussing my final week with the residency director, it was agreed that some intensification in spirit life would be wise. So beginning tomorrow, I will work in the mornings, and spend the afternoons and evenings until Vespers at the hermit's log cabin nearest the monastery. And on the final days, I will spend at least one overnight retreat at the monastic hermitage high in the mountains (a jeep trip plus a half hour walk from here). The hermit was delighted that I would be sharing "his" hermitage.

135

He prepared me by sharing observations concerning the individual habits of elk and porcupine at the hermitage salt lick and his wistful fantasies about British Columbia. "That's about the only wilderness left—and even that is a matter of time. What's a person to do when he can't breathe anymore?"

Thursday, August 24

Fr. "F" asked me to do the Prayers of the Faithful on Sunday, so that our final Sunday Eucharist could be a kind of con-celebration.

As we processed eggs I asked the prior what he does on a retreat. His answer was firm and immediate: "As little as possible." Very helpful. His advice to me was to take no books—there is a Bible there. Then you will not be tempted not "to be."

I knew he was right. I planned my afternoons accordingly. After None, armed with one jelly sandwich, an orange, a peach, a thermos of orange juice, one pencil, and one piece of paper, I started out for the hermit's hut. What was to follow was highly significant. I started out at my usual goal-oriented pace. But it finally dawned on me that I wasn't really going anyplace, perhaps for the first time in my life, so there was certainly no hurry to get there. Seemed logical. So I began "wandering," picking up a rock here, watching a ground squirrel there, and smelling a wildflower somewhere in the middle. It startled me that I could not remember when I had been utterly alone for twenty-four hours. Even in being alone I was always doing something—reading, writing, backpacking. My aloneness has been interior, and well established has been the presence of guilt over doing "nothing." Perhaps it was college that solidified the pattern—there was always another paper, another book, another something to be done. To "catch up" was always the flavor of "being." In graduate school it was the interminable dissertation to be done, or to do penance for. I remember during marriage the echo, "While you're sitting there doing nothing, will you . . .?"

Yet even without such "interruptions," it still was not doing nothing—the TV was on, the Sunday paper, or a book in hand.

All of this flooded my mind as I walked slowly nowhere. I have never really experienced having nothing to do. What an awareness. The scene in Faulkner's *The Bear* became graphic. The boy enters the wilderness to find the bear, but the bear never shows himself. Only when the boy sheds the symbols of civilization one by one, only when he is vulnerable and one with the earth, only then does the bear appear. I slipped off the one obviously remaining crutch, putting my watch in my pocket. I saw the hut but kept going, through the aspens, up the valley, and then I saw ahead the avalanched mountain with water coming from a spring halfway up. Crawling under bushes, up ravines, over cliffs, I came to where I could see that scarred mountain and the valley below. With a stick I dug out a flat space just large enough for my fanny—and there I sat. I have no idea how long. Halfway toward, and halfway from—suspended. Flies, Water trickle. Breeze in aspens. Cattle far below. Clouds ... Clouds ... Clouds. And when it was time to go (whatever that meant), I went a different way. I dreamed and found where I would build my hermit's shack—in an aspen grove in a finger canyon, overlooking "Silver Mountain." I had a hard time just being, without fantasizing—building, caring for, reverencing the earth. But the earth seemed to fantasize back, as the aspens were hinting a yellow and the oaks a red.

The hermit's hut was very primitive, a rearing station for flies; but it was proud, with just about the brightest red door imaginable. It was friend.

Friday, August 25

It is staying a bit darker each morning now. I felt unsettled as I tried to prepare for prayer in the chapel. But as I was trying, without much success, I was suddenly wrapped in a calm. It was beautiful, until the bells rang for Lauds. So simple, so gift-like.

During this second afternoon that I was to have alone, I was asked to take one of the monks to town. My homily on Sunday may have been the trigger, but he shared with me the dangers he saw of domesticating "Trappism" through its contacts with "Aspenism." "We need distance in order to be ourselves, yet we need 'benefactors' in order to make this possible." "What does it mean that we only wear our cowls for two offices a day, and prefer in our relations with outside persons to wear their kind of clothes?" "I came here because I didn't want to 'make it' by playing the games of that world; but I'm fearful lest without knowing it I let myself be wooed into only a slightly different variation of the same game." Something of this agony seemed symbolized in the journey of Br. David who had visited us. He had wanted for so long to find a monastery radically committed to the Rule of St. Benedict; he kept being disappointed. Yet in the present freedom he has to create his own monastic context he is entering into such sympathetic dialogue with non-Christian religions that the emphasis falls upon the common experience rather than on the disciplined contrast. The inclusivity of love and the toleration that is neither hot nor cold but lukewarm—that is the subtle difference that seems to be eating at us everywhere.

This evening the doe and her two fawns came to the garth for Vespers. But what is to happen to their trust when hunting season comes? Over the months here killing of any kind is becoming intolerable, yet it has no seeming end—cattle, wildflowers, life itself is enfolded in and enfolded by death. I am convinced by the joy of living that death is an enemy, an alien intruder. The doe is outside my window, carefully watching what I write.

Saturday, August 26

Today there came a call from Michigan; friends of the monastery informed us—a new Pope. The name was utterly unknown, sounding like a heavyweight boxing contender. We ran for the latest *Time* magazine to see if we should sigh or cheer. He was not even listed; what a helpless feeling. Later someone found one paragraph in another journal that referred to him as a compromise candidate who "opposed Communists." That gave us little encouragement. I wonder how many of us are best known by what we are against, rather than what we are for. So a simple objective note appeared on the bulletin board: "Luciani is Pope John Paul I." And so among the Prayers of the Faithful: "We remember when once a man whom no one knew was made a Pope that no one will forget; for such a miracle, one more time, now with Pope John Paul I, let us pray to the Lord."

My afternoon for silence was again taken—this time for errands such as tomatoes, termite spray, and Bavarian cake. All but the spray is for the farewell party tomorrow. After Vespers, I walked the empty cloister to my cell. "To walk the cloister" —that is a phrase that speaks deeply. The feel of walking there at daybreak, or at sunset, or perhaps best of all at night, with only candles to the left, and stars to the right.

Sunday, August 27

A compromise has been worked out. My retreat will be in two parts, so that I can participate in the farewell party this afternoon as well as help in the egg processing tomorrow morning. A jeep will take me to the high hermitage; a bicycle, hopefully, will get me back. So a half hour after Mass, the prior and I were bouncing up a rough road to McCartney Mesa. This is really the high country, with only the peaks higher. McCartney, it is said, lived with his two daughters in the cabin which is now the hermitage. The girls rode horseback to school each morning, a one room affair, now boarded up but still standing near the monastery. The cabin has the clear vibrations of much living, of time, and of depth. Fr. "E" had told me that the vibrations here would be warm and solid, because "several of us have had life-changing experiences there." The monks speak reverently of this place. The Abbot has been so particular about the use of the hermitage that the novice has been restricted thus far to staying two nights.

When Br. "H" drove off, I sat on the grass and looked around. The cabin was in an aspen grove, enclosed with a log fence. The mountains surround one for 180°, and on the horizon stretches the continental divide. A cold mountain stream makes enticing sounds in front, imitating the wind in the trees behind. Eventually, I used the bicycle to explore the mesa, even though it freaked out the cows to see a man with round orange legs. To the East is the steep drop-off into the valley, to the south the peaks of Haystack, Daly and Capital, to the west "Silver Mountain," and to the north the drop-off to isolated wooded meadows. The irrigated grass was lush, and the cattle as contented as I. I searched the dump for history in bottles and pails, and the dates and names preserved by aspen bark writing. On the far corner of the mesa I discovered a duplicate of the cabin drawn long ago in the bark, with a thick "X" crossing it out, and a large "No" beneath. Could it have been the hidden rebellion of a McCartney girl, drawn to despair by the long winters?

Inside the one-room cabin was a fireplace, kerosene heater, bed, table, two chairs, and a primitive altar by the front window. Most light would come from two kerosene lamps, but the most interesting light would be from the paschal candle of a former year. There was a Bible, signed by a Br. Augustine, August 1966—I wonder where he is now and if he cares where his Bible is, or remembers. The walls were bare to the exposed 5" square beams structuring the sides, except for a cross, and three statements. The first two were by e. e. cummings: "I've traveled all alone through the forest of wonder," and "Seeker of truth, follow no path. All paths lead where truth is here." The third was by Charlie Brown: "When you're really lonely, peanut butter sticks to the roof of your mouth." I peeled a banana, picked in neo-colonialized Latin America to be eaten high in the mountains of North America—incredible connectedness. To my surpise the door, though faded, was red; what is it with hermits and red doors?

My next hour resulted from coming outside and finding nowhere to sit. Who can image doing nothing without a bench? Piled against the cabin were timbers; so three timbers and two logs later there was a bench under the aspens. But this only started me. Four more timbers later and there was a new bridge over a ditch leading to the porch. And in picking up scattered brick, there first came into being a pair of steps from the side of the porch down; and from the remainder came an outdoor fireplace, just right for the next fishfry where I will not be. I sat down and thought—was I doing all of this in order to escape being? Yet I loved every minute of it. Was I leaving my mark? Or was it deeper? It seems that out of the encounter of nature and self comes a craving to create, to bring a new order, almost in spite of myself. I walked as I thought, ending up at the stream, and it happened again. Before realizing that I was doing anything, I was in the process of damming up the water, laughing as it kept finding weak spots in the breast. It got about a foot deep and maybe six feet square. Just right for wading and splashing—which I did, like a little boy. That was what was going on—sheer fun. It was a kind of "doing" that was "being." It was clearly play. Perhaps play writ large is the microcosm of work. The pioneer who had lived here had done precisely the sorts of things that I had been doing. But when one's life depends on them, the play takes on a deadly seriousness. It becomes, as it were, a game "for keeps." I remember as a boy when in our play that point of seriousness was reached. In a way it was the point of the "fall."

I became aware of how silence is not silent—there are flies (always), the birds, the wind, sound everywhere. And aloneness is not lonely. In fact, as I write this, there are five cow faces through the fence, keeping me closely supervised. There is life everywhere. My bare feet are touching it; it is buzzing around my head; it is crawling on this notebook; it is overhead.

Then, as though to render this whole experience absurd, a motorcycle bounded over the ridge and brought the rider for a talk—a rancher, checking irrigation ditches. "Not many of us left," he said. "If things keep up, there won't be any of us. It's just that I was born here and I can't bring myself to give it up.

The land becomes part of you, even if you have to starve. Don't know where it's all headed, but it sure doesn't look good."

A quiet lunch—no hurry. Unconsciously, I picked up a six-month-old newspaper in the wood box. A Denver *Catholic Register*. Christianity is such a weird business—so much there, yet it gets so twisted, until it is upside down. "Formerly liberal theologian calls the request of women for ordination 'an irrational manifestation of self-defeating feminism ...' He attacked feminists who 'do not see any other means for making women equal of men than through the masculinization of women.'" Meanwhile, back at the Pentagon, the Berrigans were arrested for their taste in exterior decorating. It was blood red, evidently. And back still further in Chicago, Cardinal Cody was praising Mayor Daley as "a man of the people" and "a great Christian." Nothing is simple, not even here in the mountains.

It was time already to leave! I heard a sound on the porch. It was interesting to discover that my patience could outlast the sound. The squirrel moved, and I saw her before the reverse. Onto the bicycle, and into an unbelievable trip down the mountain. A half hour later, a bit tense and somewhat selectively bruised, I put on the brakes, barely, at the ranch house door, just in time for the party. What a transition.

It was a very intimate gathering, a kind of reveling in friendship—small groupings, recollection time, with laughter constituting the litany of thanksgiving. It is interesting how with time one can laugh at almost anything—and redeem it. As people gathered, it was almost like a eucharistic offering —cake from one source, champagne from another; Br. "C." contributed his famous spaghetti sauce, Fr. "F" his favorite drink expertise. But it was Br. "H." who did the royal act—thirty-three of the finest monk-caught trout this side of the continental divide. Golden brown crust of cornmeal and egg. As we ate and shared and laughed, it was crazy but for a flash I recalled the resurrection fish meal of Christ and his disciples, when they could look back and laugh: "We did it!" Many thoughts flooded my mind that evening. I remembered fondly the community's favorite phrase—how several monks will look at each other, smile, and say, "Let's go for it."

Bread, wine, fish, spaghetti, and Vespers. Psalms, as always, and good music. Everyone was mellow, so mellow that it was surprising that anything so unplanned could come together. But it did. Each person made some contribution. I was asked to find a Scripture reading. I chose Revelation 21—a new heaven and a new earth—closing with the hope that this monastery shall be a foretaste of God's promised newness. But the "real" Eucharist began with an informal introit: "There's ice cream and cake in the kitchen!" Br. "C." was "celebrant," complete with battered hat, spaghetti-decorated pink tie, and phony cigar. And as though by prescribed liturgical rhythm, we moved into the oral history phase. Almost all of us knew every story already, and who would tell it. It was predictable, but it didn't matter. It was as funny as ever. Familiarity seemed to enhance rather than subtract.

Nearing the end, Fr. "E." began sharing his love of stars; and before long we were all outside watching Venus do exactly what he had told her to do.

Later, I walked alone the cloisters to my cell. It had a feel of being the last time, but also the feel of being home—almost.

Monday, August 28

After egg processing, Br. "H." drove me back to the high hermitage. We have had a running joke that before I left he would show me some elk. For as long as I can remember, from childhood, I have wanted to see an elk, but never have. His parting words were: "I hope the elk visit you this time."

This was the feast day of one of my favorites, St. Augustine. In him many of the paradoxes of my own being are evidenced. Passion and intellect, worldly and ascetic, despairing and visionary, Christocentric and universal, love-hate with the Church, prophetic and pastoral, arrogant and gentle, in love with the concretes of the earth and ecstatic with the cosmos bathed in promise, plagued by trust and by evil as intrinsic to the way things are. In my pack were fruit, several battered sandwiches, some orange juice, boiled eggs, and a small bottle of wine for Eucharist (contributed by Br. "C.," who also sent a little yellow candle in a blue glass cup).

I settled down on the new bench, looking out at the mountains. Three things came to me, all at once, seemingly related. I remembered Br. "A" at morning Mass, breaking down during intercessions as he thanked God for Fr. "F," his "brother-friend" who returned today to his own monastery. He ended with the weak request (more like a hint) that God might let them see each other again, someday. And I sensed again deeply within me the passion to create. The image of God within us must be that of the Creator. I was swept as I looked at the panorama of God's artistry and how it tugged on me. And third, that morning as I was returning my books to the library shelves, I saw one by Janov on *The Primal Scream*. The introduction described several cases in which patients, speaking of and then as if to their parents, had emerge from them an "inexplicable but primal scream." Only after its release could reintegration begin occurring. As I reflect, I know that it is true. There has been in me for as long as I can remember the rising guttural need to scream, but it is a cosmic scream. This is why in literature I have been drawn to Camus and Ivan Karamazov. So while the focus of the primal scream is clearly with parents, through them it reverberates to the Cosmic Parent. Life always seems to verge on the insane, the "dirty trickness," the sound and fury, the joke. And what I am sensing at this moment is that in Jesus Christ there occurred the primal scream in behalf of us all: "My God, my God, why hast thou forsaken me?" But if that cross is thereby the scream in the soul of Being Itself, is it not also somehow the promise that is resurrection, for God is with us in eternal struggle against the Void? With such companion eyes one can dare see through the tears a new universe to be reveled in, as a child, a guest, an heir, a creator in the becoming of creation.

I arose, feeling washed, and walked everywhere—and

found myself talking to everything: squirrels, a red root by a stream, mountains, leaves, a particularly courageous tree, the velvety bark of a large bush that no doubt was growing just for me. All took on the feel of companion. The stream particularly had the propensity to talk back. I sat there, fascinated by its running, falling, restless movement. I played with its sounds, and my head marked the rhythm.

I looked for elk, among the trees, in the meadows, everywhere. There were only rabbits (big ones, however).

The world began preparing for sleep. The earth lets one sense what to do and when. It is a matter of feeling the "fitting." The monks had told me that the trees at the edge of the mesa had been cut down so that at night a lantern hung in the front window could be seen miles away at the monastery as a call for help. That had been comforting. But now there was no need. I was at peace. As I walked back at sunset to the cabin, everything seemed to have a quiet and important insignificance. Nothing mattered because everything did. There was an overwhelming sense of gentleness, so that one walked quietly on tiptoes in the grass and on the needles, as if not to disturb anything.

I felt the sloped floors of the cabin, each "wave"with a different story. I walked from window to window, not wanting to miss anything. It had been a cloudless day, so I expected no sunset. But out of the front window, I saw something new for me— a reverse sunset. In the East, mist and beginning clouds had formed over the continental divide. And the setting sun, which I could not see because of the trees, was playing on the clouds. I had to go outside, and in the pleasant, warm breeze, they put on their show. I looked not up at the clouds, but out on them, and sensed the world get drowsy.

And then, out in the front meadow I saw some deer. It was getting dark now, as I quietly walked the edge of the mesa through the trees, until I was within fifty yards of them. As I sat in the dusk to watch, I recognized in sheer amazement that they were not deer—they were huge. They were elk—six of them, two of which were young, rolling and chasing each other. In the wind they would occasionally jerk their heads, with rack erect, just listening. And as darkness began in earnest, it seemed as if the whole woods were stage wings giving up their actors. Grey-like images floated out, stood, and moved, with only the sound of their occasional breathing in the silence. I was in the midst of a whole herd of elk, surrounding me. I can't imagine how many.

I made my way back through the dark mesa come alive. Washing in the stream, I was struck powerfully by how each act was taking on the feel of a sacramental. Inside, I lit the paschal candle, and, from it, a fire. Watching the life of a fire in a quiet place—it is like watching wanton water or restless grass or oceans or wildlife; they are all, it would seem, of the same genre—the spacious little things.

It seemed right for the Eucharist now, for a more "formal" consecration of the elements already abundantly offered. Burlap on the table by the front window, a Bible, candles, chalice and paten. Before me, somewhere out there, the elk as communicants, the fire behind me reflecting on the window glass, and above us the bare outline of the mountains in the last fingers of light, hesitating. And then several strokes of lightning on the continental divide. Sheer ecstasy.

> Blessed are you, Lord, God of all creation.
> Through your goodness we have this . . . earth to offer.
> Blessed be God forever . . .
> Father, accept this offering from your whole family . . .
> in memory . . . in fact . . . in hope .

Then to bed, by the fire. Crackling. Warm. Complete.

Tuesday, August 29

Several monks had expressed disappointment that I had been told to be back for morning Lauds. But as I rode down the

Rocky Mountains on a bicycle at sunrise, it seemed absurdly right.

The next day or two are blurred, as one might expect. Doing uncompleted jobs, giving each tree a final watering, experiencing each thing as if for the last time. A matter of returning countless "acquaintances" to their forgotten places—wire stretchers, gloves, grasscutters, hose washers. It is a kind of bequeathing them for someone else to carry on.

There is a sadness, as I write this two hours before my final Eucharist. Everything has a sadness, as even the aspen trees on the hills are beginning to turn yellow, commencing what my hermit friend calls the "melancholy of autumn."

Barth was right when he said that the resurrection makes sense only to those so deeply in love with this earth that they are overcome by the thought of leaving it.

Last evening Fr. "E." saw me watering trees on the hill and walked up to be with me. A final thanks, gratitude, friendship, perhaps again. The Abbot asked for a final talk after Vespers. This time he shared something of himself, how touched he was on his trip to the commune by the respect given each religious tradition—observing the Jewish sabbath, praying as the sun set, sufi dancing, various scriptures. The unity of all in an active tolerance, a curiosity and openness both to learn and to share. For a moment he let his fantasies for an ecumenical monasticism begin to emerge. Then he turned to me. His concern was for my transition, for continued growth, for what I would call "faithfulness." His conclusion was that it would depend upon a disciplined life. Although it is hard to believe that one could lose all of this, no doubt it too will pass, without the *habitus*, the disciplined intention. Together we decided upon periods of morning and evening contemplative prayer, Scripture as meditation, and frequent Eucharist—simple things, obvious things.

Whatever else, I leave with one important difference from when I came. I have been there. I am on the other side. And although I recross the river, it will now be as an alien resident.

At Eucharist, Fr. "E's" prayer was important: "For the

seeds planted by the Spirit in Brother Paul, that they may grow to fullness in all their beauty, and for the seeds planted by Paul in us and in our community; may we be the instruments of their growth in all their richness—let us pray to the Lord." An embrace of peace with each monk as a final goodbye, the common loaf, the common cup, the final blessing as hope, and I left— quickly.

Down the road by car, with a final look back. But I cheated. Instead of turning north at the intersection, toward the main highway and "home," I turned south. To the end of the blacktop, to the end of the negotiable dirt road—a two-mile hike. And then I was standing for a final time at the beaver ponds, looking down at the wilderness and out at towering Capital Peak. Whatever happens, at least I know that she will be there, for a long time.

Sunday, September 3

Two hot days crossing the plains, and into the city. But I made an unfortunate calculation. From silence into the inner city is shock enough but to arrive at full moon on a Saturday night is insanity. I was tired, but it was to little avail—trains, police cars, the interstate, fire trucks, bars filling, bars emptying. And at 3:30 A.M. I was awakened, no longer by bells, but by drunken yells. Then the shatter of glass. Once ... twice ... three times. Out of bed, early morning rising, but this time with a difference. Down three flights. Our glass front door was in pieces, all over the hallway. People were gathering in the street. It was a good reunion with "the folks" again, but I had not planned my re-entry this way.

A neighbor had seen it. A young man without a shirt, on drugs, evidently, swinging a machete. First Robbi's house, then mine, and last the Herndons' next door. We talked for an hour, a genuine togetherness of ghetto folk, knowing "we're in it together," at least because "there's no way out."

Later in the morning, as I was repairing the damage, the neighbor across the street came over with a "coming home present." "Just a little while ago," he said with pride, "I moved my bed into the front room, right by the window. My loaded rifle is on the sill. If anyone messes with your place, it will be the last time."

This evening the violence took the form of a heavy thunderstorm. A social worker friend living in the next block called. She wanted to walk in the rain. She was anxious to hear what I had "discovered," and in turn she shared her own longing for—for what? I guess for a meaning that is beyond but is within the changing. "We've been working here six years now, you and I, and what do we have to show for it?" We discussed each house as we walked by—pregnancy, jail, wife-beating, dealing, abortion, unemployment, glue ... We kept waiting for a house signaling success, as the rain came down so hard that we laughed, absurdly. Few were other than temporary respite. She asked the obvious, but I heard it as my own voice: "Then why do we do it?" We walked in silence. She would be married by spring, and gone.

Later, over Bach and coffee, musing over folks here never having a chance, I remembered Chesterton's images for the world. Sometimes, he said, it's like an ogre's castle that must be taken by storm; other times it is like a woodcutter's cottage into which one comes as home. Yes. But somehow life has never let me experience them in separation.

Sheila, the intelligent high school dropout, came over: "What the hell you been doin' in a monastery?" "Just being," I said. "Kinda like having a six pack?" she responded. "Yes, I guess its kind of like that, if you're with a friend."

This morning's mail had a letter from my father. His surgical fight against cancer had failed.

Like life, journals don't end—they stop. The real "province on the river's far side" is the craving soul. Whoever is bitten by it will not rest in its testing of the darkness. My monastic experience brought no certainty, one way or another. It was far worse. It brought an intoxication for the darkness itself, in all its graciously shattering antinomies—the joy of the universally sorrowful, the unspeakable gift just of surviving, being acceptingly unreconciled, longing for the Mystery no longer doubted, as the cold emptiness has somehow persisted as the warm silence.